Be Good

Grandpa's Guidebook to a Life Well Lived

Allison Katie

Edited by Carly Beth

Love Your Legacy Publishing—Paoli, PA
ISBN: 979-8-218-56418-6
Library of Congress Control Number: 2024926244
Title: *Be Good: Grandpa's Guidebook to a Life Well Lived*
Author: Allison Inch
Digital distribution | 2024
Paperback | 2024

Published in the United States by New Book Authors Publishing

Dedication

In loving memory of my grandfather, Ed Wagner, whose legacy will forever live on in these pages and in our hearts.

Table of Contents

Preface vii
Rule #1: Work Hard................................. 1
Rule #2: Play Hard 9
Rule #3: "It is What it Is" 14
Rule #4: Nothing Goes to Waste 20
Rule #5: If it's Broken, Fix It 27
Rule #6: Smile 32
Rule #7: Talk Less, Listen More 39
Rule #8: Stay Humble 45
Rule #9: Be Patient 50
Rule #10: Live Simply 61
Rule #11: Family Comes First 70
Rule #12: Choose Love 82
Rule #13: Enjoy the Ride.......................... 93
Epilogue 101
Rule #14: Be Good 101

Preface

How often have you heard children say, "I have the best Nana and Pop Pop in the world!" or how many greeting cards have you seen addressed to the greatest grandparents ever? It is true - there are a lot of amazing grandparents out there, and good reason for many to assume that their Grandma and Grandpa are better than all others. Well, I am no exception to this as I, too, have always believed that I have the best grandparents, specifically grandfather, ever. Unfortunately, though, he is no longer with us, but still not a day goes by that I don't think about him - his genuine smile, his warm-hearted hugs, and his gentle yet confident demeanor that has always served as the guide for our family. As we gathered together in the days leading up to his funeral, as often happens, countless stories were shared as we remembered all the qualities that made him so special. I had always known that Grandpa was an incredible man, but as we sat around reminiscing, I was filled with an even greater sense of awe and admiration as I came to realize the extent of his legacy.

They say you become wiser with age, learning from the past and gaining a better understanding of the ways of the world, and Grandpa was no exception to this old adage. I only knew him for the last 30 years of his life, so by this time, his life experiences had taught him a lot; however, I believe he had possessed this wisdom well before his time. I don't have a firsthand account of his early years, but based on the stories I've heard from many, I believe his character reflected this wisdom most of his life. Maybe it was his humble upbringing, a small-town mindset, or his steadfast faith that shaped his character, but whatever it was, I am forever grateful for the example he provided. I learned a lot from Grandpa over the years, and although I know I will probably never achieve the bar that he has set, I have developed a better sense of the way I want to live as well as the qualities that I really appreciate in others.

In my eyes, Grandpa was the perfect person. I know, I know, nobody is perfect, but in all honesty, he was pretty damn close. For those who were blessed enough to know Grandpa, I'm sure they would share the same sentiment as what his family recognized in him. He was a kind, caring, and selfless man who made everyone around him feel so incredibly loved. The positive effect he had on others was undeniable, but unfortunately, his impact was limited. Other than attending his grandchildren's sporting events, he rarely crossed the county line, so that is the reason I am writing this book - to extend his reach so that more people can experience how simple yet powerful his presence was in this world. It is my hope that as I share the values and guiding principles that Grandpa embodied, you will come to realize how his life truly left a lasting impression on all those around him. And maybe, hopefully, you might look to incorporate some of "Grandpa's Rules" into your own life as well, because I believe that this world would be a much better place if there were just a few more people like him out there.

Rule #1
Work Hard

Grandpa grew up in a small town in central Pennsylvania where most people earned a living through farming or other "blue collar" professions, working long hours and performing physically-demanding jobs. He also grew up in a generation where kids were expected to help out on the farm or around the house as soon as they were able, so a strong work ethic was instilled in him at a very early age. I'm not sure if it was this upbringing alone, his time in the military, or it might simply have been a special quality he possessed that fueled his work ethic, but what I do know is that Grandpa was one of the strongest and hardest working men I have ever known.

After getting out of the military, Grandpa worked at numerous jobs throughout the years. His primary professions were carpentry and construction, which are hard work in and of themselves, but he also held positions in other trades including maintenance and custodial services as well as working as a gas station attendant at one point. He did whatever was needed to provide for his wife and five children, and most of the time, that meant working at least two jobs and often moonlighting on the side to make ends meet.

In addition to the countless hours he put in each

week at his various jobs, he also spent a lot of his "free" time working hard to create a loving home for his family. This not only included household chores such as mowing the lawn or chopping firewood, but (after his first two children were born), Grandpa somehow found the time to single-handedly build their family's first home. Several years after that, then, he also restored and expanded the family farmhouse where my grandmother had grown up, eventually moving his own family there, and remarkably, this is where he and Grandma would spend the remainder of their years together.

Whether he was working multiple jobs to make ends meet, taking care of things around the house, or even building homes, Grandpa recognized his role as leader and provider for his family, and he went above and beyond to fulfill that role. He worked incredibly hard day after day to make sure his family never went without, not only financially, but Grandpa was always there to offer guidance, support, and unconditional love whenever it was needed as well.

Even after retirement, Grandpa's immense work ethic continued into the later years of his life. Until I was able to remember much of anything, Grandpa would have been in his late sixties or early seventies and even then, I remember him always working on something. He continued to keep busy with projects in his workshop, tending to the yard and garden, and fixing odds and ends around the farm. And when my Uncle Scot opened a bike shop in town, Grandpa also started helping out there most days of the week, learning yet another trade to add to his tool belt.

I remember watching him in his later years and

wondering how much pain he must have been in. His swollen, arthritic hands and hunched-over back made certain things difficult, but it never stopped him, and he rarely ever asked anyone for help. He was still climbing ladders, bringing logs in to load the wood stove, and getting down on his hands and knees to pick the vegetables from his garden. Maybe it was his pride or possibly a bit of stubbornness, but I do know he recognized the value of hard work as well as independence. He never had the benefit of having things handed to him, and he learned early on that if you want something, you're going to have to work for it. You should never expect anything in life - if you truly want something, you need to pursue it. I think he also understood that the harder you work for something, the more you will appreciate it. He put his heart and soul into everything he did because he knew the end result was worth every bit of effort.

Growing up in a small, rural town as Grandpa had, I was surrounded by many others with the same mentality, so the importance of hard work was taught to me at a young age as well. Life has now led me away from the countryside, though, and landed me in an upper-class, suburban area where opportunity and success appear much more accessible and abundant. As a transplant from the "middle of nowhere," as many like to call it, I have heard every joke there is about hillbillies and rednecks riding their horse-and-buggies and living off the land. I have been teased about my love of country music and the slow drawl that occasionally slips out as I am speaking. When this happens, though, I simply roll my eyes because I have heard it all before. I understand that the country way of living may not seem very appealing to those who haven't experienced it, but truthfully, I am incredibly grateful for this type of upbringing and the values it has instilled in me, a strong work ethic being one.

I have been blessed in many areas of my life - a loving and supportive group of family and friends, a job that I truly enjoy, and opportunities that have allowed me to grow in both my career and life in general. I'm not saying that I deserve all that I have, but I do know that without a strong work ethic and the grace of God, I would certainly not be where I am today. And honestly, I find so much more satisfaction in knowing that I worked hard for these things rather than them being handed to me. I believe there is a lot to be said about earning something rather than it simply being given to you. The fulfillment that comes from putting in the work - the blood, tears, and sweat - and seeing a dream come to life, I believe makes it all worth it in the long run. I recognize that hard work does require more time and energy and is not nearly as appealing as something that offers instant gratification, but hard work is what will allow you to excel and ultimately, achieve your full potential. Now don't get me wrong, I'm not going to turn down a good thing because I have not earned it on my own, but I do think we need to remember the value of hard work as well as the satisfaction that comes with it.

In the upscale neighborhood where I now reside, many people earn their living through business, finance, and other white-collar professions - a drastic change from what I was used to. It is a very affluent community in which many people have experienced great opportunity and success. I have no doubt that many of them have put in a lot of hard work in order to get them to where they are today, and these individuals deserve all the success and prosperity that comes with it. To be able to build something and then pass it on to future generations is a special privilege, and I commend people for the ingenuity, dedication, and hard work that leads to this level of achievement. However, I have also witnessed the sense of entitlement that sometimes comes with it. I am surrounded by people who have been given great opportunities such as attending amazing schools, private lessons in whatever sport or art they are pursuing, or a role in the family business after they've graduated from a prestigious college. Far too often, though, it seems these blessings are expected rather than appreciated.

Unfortunately, we are not all born into the comfort and privilege of wealth and financial security, but there are so many stories out there of individuals who came from nothing, but through a lot of hard work, were able to make a name for themselves. We can only play the cards we are dealt, so rather than dwelling on what we don't have and complaining about the advantages of others, we need to focus on what we can do in order to create the life we want. If you aren't happy with where you are in life, hard work is what will help you change your situation. Yes, the road may be more difficult with mountains standing in the way, but I think looking back on all of those obstacles that you were able to overcome through hard work and perseverance, only makes the success that much sweeter.

Currently, I see "help wanted" signs everywhere. Businesses are closing down because they cannot find workers, stores are cutting back hours because they are short-staffed, and restaurants can no longer accommodate full-capacity because they do not have enough servers. Schools are under-staffed as well, lacking people in vital positions such as custodians, bus drivers, substitute teachers, and aides, and talking with others, the shortage of workers seems to be a problem in many professions. Considering the number of people in this country who are capable of working, I do question why there seems to be such a limited work force. To a certain extent, I believe some people may be feeling overworked, underpaid, and underappreciated for the jobs they do which is certainly a problem that needs to be addressed. Unfortunately, though, I think an issue our society faces is that a number of people simply don't want to put the time and effort into a steady job. Rather, they prefer the freedom and flexibility that comes with other means of income whether it is unemployment or disability checks, playing the stocks, gambling, or even illegal means. Furthermore, social media now offers countless money-making opportunities from becoming an "influencer" to creating accounts that people must pay to follow. For younger generations that have been raised on social media, this "line of work" is much more appealing than monotonous nine-to-five shiftwork. Now, I do recognize that these means typically require less time and effort as well as offer the opportunity for fame or a big pay day which is certainly enticing, but where would society be if we all chose to seek the "quick buck" or the easy road for our means of financial income?

I don't know about you, but I don't want to live in a world where no one is willing to put in the hard work that it takes to generate meaningful progress. The houses we live in, the roads we drive on, and every building we enter were constructed by those who were willing to put in the long hours and perform the strenuous labor that is needed to maintain our country's infrastructure. And it's not just the physically-demanding jobs that require hard work. Professions in the medical field, education, public service, and many, many others are demanding as well, and I know that I am certainly grateful for all those who do these jobs and do them well. Society would not be able to function without these individuals, and they certainly do not get enough credit for the work they do. In my opinion, these are the people that deserve the spotlight for their efforts and success because I think if we gave these hard-working individuals the recognition and appreciation they are worthy of, I believe others would be more encouraged to do the same.

When I think about the people I work alongside, I know that I am especially grateful for those who work hard and handle their responsibilities without relying on others to do their work for them. Even more so, though, I have come to appreciate those who always put their best foot forward as this level of work ethic not only leads to good things for that individual, but it also benefits everyone around them. I know it is difficult and can be discouraging when others are not giving the same level of effort, but I do believe people will respect and appreciate you that much more when you consistently work hard and put forth your best effort. Furthermore, that working mentality and the habits that come with it will only lead to greater opportunity and more success in the future because when you put in the work, you will assuredly move forward in your career and your life.

Grandpa was an extremely hard-working man, and as a result, he was able to build a comfortable life for him, his wife, and their five children. They were not rich by any means, but they always had what they needed and never went without. Yes, that hard work may have taken a toll on his body over the years, but I don't think Grandpa ever regretted the career path he chose. Rather, I think he took pride in the work he did, content in knowing that his honest day's work was not only providing for his family, but it was also benefiting the community. He certainly was not one to sit back and complain about his situation or expect others to do the work for him. He recognized the power of hard work, knowing that if you want something, *you* need to be the one to go out and get it. Nothing is out of reach if you are simply willing to put forth the effort.

Life Lesson #1:

Don't be afraid of a little hard work; it's what makes the world go round. The extra effort you put in will always be worth it, and the joy you will find in achieving your goals through that hard work will be that much sweeter.

Rule #2
Play Hard

It may seem as though Grandpa was the "all work and no play" type, but he certainly knew how to have a good time too. I always appreciated his ability to have a little fun when the opportunity would present itself, and he definitely had the "stay young" mentality. In fact, just a few days before he passed away, he made the comment to my mom and me saying, "You're not old until you're 89, right?" He had been 88 at the time.

Grandpa never let his age determine what he could and couldn't do, and in all honesty, I believe he lived to defy age, intentionally seeking ways to prove that age was just a number and should never limit you. He never let someone tell him that he was too old for something, but if they did, in his mind it was a challenge, and he wasn't going to stop until he had proved them wrong. At one point, his doctor told him that he should begin thinking about assisted living because he and my grandmother were getting older and were not as mobile as they once had been. Needless to say, that doctor never saw my grandparents again because they immediately switched to another practitioner. He was certainly not about to let a doctor tell him he was too old to live on his own.

I remember one Christmas in which we were all gathered at my grandparents' house for our traditional get together. After the presents had been opened and dinner was eaten, we were busy cleaning up in the kitchen, washing and drying the mountains of dishes, finding the right size containers for the abundance of leftovers, and putting the extra chairs and tables away. Everyone had their job, so nobody had been paying much attention to where Grandpa was, but just as we were finishing up, he came walking through the front door, bundled up in his winter coat and carrying a pair of ice skates.

My mom said to him, "Where have you been?"

To which he replied, "I just wanted to be able to say that I could still ice skate when I was 80 years old."

That was Grandpa - never letting his age stop him from doing what he enjoyed.

His love of bike-riding and the miles upon miles that he would ride is another example of how he refused to let his age slow him down. He discovered a passion for this activity in his later years, and as a result, he would take any opportunity he could get to ride around on that bike. For Grandpa's 80th birthday, our family celebrated by riding twenty-six miles, a convoy of about 20 of his children, grandchildren, and great grandchildren pedaling along the trail with him. And as he crossed the makeshift finish line that we had strung across the trail at the end of the ride, he stood up, tall on the pedals, beaming with childlike joy. He was in all his glory, and I don't think he had ever been happier than in that moment.

For his 85th birthday, we biked a little over 15

miles, and although it was a shorter distance than his 80th, it was a more strenuous ride with hills and rougher terrain, but that didn't slow him down one bit. And on his 88th birthday, we kept the tradition alive, riding another 20 miles as Grandpa celebrated his birthday doing what he loved most with the people he cherished more than anything.

At his memorial service, the pastor shared a story about one of the first times he had met Grandpa who at this point was in his mid-80s. He said Grandpa was about to fix the clock on the bell tower of the church, and he had offered to show the new pastor "the ropes". When the pastor realized the only way up to that bell tower was via a steep ladder, he politely declined the tour, but much to his surprise, Grandpa proceeded to work his way up the ladder, taking it two rungs at a time no less. Not only was Grandpa still climbing to the peak of the church on occasion, but he was doing it as if he was a spry 20-year-old. This didn't surprise me though. That man was climbing up ladders and standing on step stools until the day he died. I forget who was able to capture this particular shot of Grandpa, but there is a picture of him winding up the living room clock, one foot on a small stool and his other leg propped up on the side table - not exactly the most sturdy base, but he got the job done. He was no longer tall enough to reach it without a step stool, but he sure as hell was not going to ask anyone for help.

There was another sweet picture of Grandpa that had been displayed in the kitchen, propped up on the small desk that sat in the corner. It is a photo of him riding my brother's scooter around Uncle Scot's bike shop. He has the biggest smile on his face and a twinkle in his eyes, looking just like a little kid again. It's the simple things that could bring Grandpa so much joy, and for me, that picture is always a special reminder of his passion for life. No matter how old he got, he was always open to trying something new or doing things that most people would have let their age deter them from doing. He truly lived each day to the fullest, embracing each and every moment as a blessing that he needed to make the most of.

Looking back on Grandpa's desire to defy age and not let it confine him, I have come to appreciate this mentality more and more. It is a mindset that doesn't just pertain to age, though. Whether it is your gender, race, sexuality, socioeconomic status, etc., you should never let it limit what you can and cannot do. I am a true believer in the idea that you can achieve anything you set your mind to, and if it is something that you are passionate about and it makes you happy, go for it. Don't let society tell you things like "Girls can't do that" or "You'll never be able to achieve that." If people can't appreciate and respect you for chasing a dream or doing something that brings you joy, then their opinion really doesn't matter. It is your life, and in my opinion, your happiness is the most important thing because that is what brings you contentment and fulfillment. Even our country's Declaration of Independence states that all people are entitled to "life, liberty, and the *pursuit of happiness*." This life is not about pleasing others or trying to fit into some stereotype that society tells you is the right way to live. You have the basic human right to happiness, so don't ever let anyone or anything steal that from you.

Find what makes you happy and pursue that every single day.

Life Lesson #2:

This life is a gift and is meant to be enjoyed, so don't let yourself get so caught up in the ways of this world that you forget to have fun. You will never regret a day that was spent doing what makes *you* happy.

Rule #3
"It Is What It Is"

At the time my grandmother passed away, she and Grandpa had been married for more than 67 years. From their high school days to raising a family, and eventually seeing many of their kids and grandkids get married and have children of their own, they had been through so much together. To say he had lost the love of his life and "his everything" is an understatement. While there is no way to truly know what a grieving husband needs or how to help during a difficult time like that, it was comforting to see such a great deal of love and support pour in from so many friends and family.

However, in the midst of that whirlwind - phone calls, people dropping by with flowers and food, and planning the funeral - my aunt had realized that two of Grandpa's brothers had not reached out to share their condolences. She found this surprising and a little upsetting, but when she mentioned it to Grandpa, he simply shrugged his shoulders and responded, "It is what it is."

My aunt shared this with us later that evening because she, as did we, recognized the power of those few little words. His reaction to this situation demonstrated so much wisdom. In that moment, Grandpa knew that getting upset over his brothers' not calling would only damage his relationship with his siblings as well as bring down those around him. He knew that their small inaction should not undo eighty plus years of brotherhood. I'm sure a part of him was a little disappointed and understandably so, but again, he didn't see the need to make a big deal out of it because ultimately, it wouldn't change anything.

As I reflected on Grandpa's response to this particular situation, I realized that he had always lived his life with this type of mentality. I honestly can't remember a time when he complained about anything. He wouldn't grumble after a long day of work, knowing that he still needed to spend several hours at the farmhouse, fixing it up so that his family could eventually move in there. He wouldn't gripe when he needed to get all five children ready for bed on the nights Grandma worked at the ice cream stand, again, after an exhausting day of work for him. Rather, he always chose to focus his energy on doing what needed to be done. He knew that complaining and feeling sorry for himself would not provide for his family; instead, it would only lead to resentment and bitterness which is never good for the family dynamic or any type of relationship for that matter.

Grandpa never mentioned any of the aches or pains that he endured daily either. If his arthritis was flaring up, his back was bothering him, or even if he was experiencing chest pain, he never complained about it. He wasn't one to seek sympathy from others nor did he feel the need to push his burdens on them because he recognized that moaning about it was not going to make the fatigue or the pain go away.

Grandpa seemed to take everything in stride. His life was far from easy, but he never complained about it. No matter what needed to be done or if there was a problem to be solved, Grandpa would find a way because "it is what it is," and you just have to do the best with the cards you're dealt. He understood that there is no sense in worrying about the things out of our control or life's little inconveniences; that won't accomplish anything. Instead, sometimes you just have to "roll with the punches" as they say.

As we were planning Grandma's funeral, the director called with a pretty significant issue, or so we thought. We had all been sitting around the table after lunch, when my aunt got off the phone and explained the situation. My grandparents were always to be buried in a plot with my grandma's mother, father, and Aunt Kate. Unfortunately, though, they had already been buried in the three middle plots meaning there was only room on either end of them for Grandma and Grandpa, so they would not be able to be buried next to one another. After the initial shock of this information, it took Grandpa about thirty seconds to find a solution. He suggested that he had always wanted to be cremated so they could simply bury him above Grandma when the time came. I don't think any of us were aware that Grandpa wanted to be cremated, and we will never know if this was truly the case, but it certainly did solve the problem at hand without much fuss.

This was Grandpa. He was not one for dwelling on problems or worrying about things he couldn't change. Grandpa preferred to focus on what he could control and the things he could do to fix or at least improve a situation. I'm sure there were many times when he wished things could be different or easier, but no matter what life handed him, he continued to move forward because he knew that was the only choice he had.

I think another reason Grandpa had developed the "it is what it is" mindset is because he recognized that expecting things from others or even life in general often leads to unnecessary disappointment and frustration. Expectations seem to lead to so many arguments as well as needless resentment. For example, you might expect your spouse to automatically do something you never asked them to do, or you thought your coworker would run the reports for the meeting, or we hope our kids will do something without our guidance. Why do we assume others will meet certain expectations that we have for them when we've never communicated these things? People are who they are and just because we think they should do something or behave in a certain way, does not mean they will all of a sudden become who we would like them to be. Grandpa, though, never expected anything from anyone, and I'm sure it saved him many headaches and quite a bit of stress over the years. He always loved us unconditionally for who we were, and our actions or even inactions never changed that.

The same goes for what we expect from this life. Life isn't fair, and no matter how well we know this to be true, we still expect it to change. We expect things to be better or easier, or we think we deserve more than we have. Not only do we have unrealistic expectations about what this world owes us, but we are then so easily frustrated when things don't go our way. However, if we simply view this life for what it is rather than what we wish it to be - or if we simply love the people we love for who they are - we might avoid a lot of needless disappointment and aggravation.

In my experience, complaining never makes a situation better. I recognize that sometimes we may need to vent and get things off our chest which is completely understandable, but I've come to realize that this does nothing to change the situation that is causing the unrest. Instead, it gives that person or situation power over you, taking up room in your mind and heart and stealing your peace. So rather than dwelling on it or complaining about it, I suggest you consider whether there is anything you can do to improve the situation, and if so, do it because you will then be the one controlling the situation, not the other way around. However, if there is nothing you can do, then I think it is better to just let it go. I know that this is easier said than done, but it is honestly so refreshing when you are able to free yourself of those negative and burdensome thoughts. So my advice is don't allow others to gain that power over you - control what you can and let go of what you can't.

At the gathering that followed Grandpa's funeral, I remember his brother sharing a story of yet another "it is what it is" moment. He recounted a conversation he had had with Grandpa just a few weeks prior - a discussion about dying - and he had asked him his thoughts on the topic. I can't recall what the specific question was, but I will never forget Grandpa's straightforward response. "Well, it's not really up to us, now is it?" Grandpa was certainly good at simplifying things.

Grandpa always recognized that it's not worth worrying about things that are beyond our control, including death. This isn't to diminish the pain and heartbreak that comes from losing a loved one or any of the other countless tragedies that people experience every day, but I think it is a good reminder that so many things in life are merely out of our hands.

There are always going to be struggles in this life. Grandpa certainly experienced his fair share of it, but you would have never known by the way he lived his life. He understood more than most people that many things are out of our control and no amount of worrying or complaining is going to change anything for the better. He would simply feel what he needed to feel, and then, he would move forward because, at the end of the day, that really is the only option. I think the sooner we all realize this - that some things just are what they are - the better. Then, we will be able to focus on the things that truly matter rather than spending so much of our time and energy dwelling on the things that we simply cannot control.

Life Lesson #3:

Sometimes it just is what it is, and there is nothing you can do about it. If that's the case, let it go; otherwise, it will continue to steal your peace.

Rule #4
Nothing Goes to Waste

Grandpa was "green" before the "go green" movement had even begun, and honestly, he was on an entirely different level. Now, Grandpa's family never had much when he was growing up, and since he lived through the era of the "Great Depression," I can understand why he felt the need to reuse and recycle everything, but even when these habits were no longer necessary for survival, he continued to conserve all that he could. For example, my grandparents were notorious for reusing many products that are typically intended for a single use. Sheets of tin foil would be washed over and over again until they were worn through in places, and plastic Ziploc bags would be hand-washed, hung on the drying rack, and then placed back in the drawer to be used again. The same red Solo cups were used for every picnic, party, and family reunion for as long as I can remember, and the same can be said for the plasticware. They would even reuse their napkins, so if I was ever tasked with setting the table for dinner, I would always be sure to pull the napkins from the bottom of the pile because the two on top had more than likely been used already and would continue to be used for at least a couple more meals. They never threw away anything that still had a little use left in it.

Recycling was extremely important to Grandpa as well. If he couldn't reuse it, he made sure it was recycled in some way, shape or form. He would always take the extra time to clean out jars, bottles, and other recyclables and place them in the recycling bin rather than simply tossing them in the trash. Apparently, he would even go so far as to sort through the trash to salvage pieces of recycling as my Uncle Scot shared that he had once found Grandpa in the basement after a family reunion with the trash that had accumulated from the party spread out on the floor. He was down on his hands and knees, separating pieces of paper and plastic, ensuring that no recyclables were thrown away with the trash. I know many people try to recycle as best they can, but I've never heard of people going through the garbage in order to do so. Like I said, he took the term "green" to a whole other level.

Food certainly never went to waste in that house either. Grandpa's plate was always spotless after a meal as he would eat every last crumb he was served as well as any crumbs that remained on his children's or grandchildren's plates. However, he has taught us well because we usually don't leave anything on our plates either - if you look around the table after a family meal, there is hardly a scrap of food to be seen. If there was any extra food remaining in the serving dishes after a meal, though, it would be packed in plastic containers and placed in the refrigerator to be eaten as leftovers in the coming days. Even if it was only enough to barely fill a little butter dish (yes, the butter dishes were reused as food containers), it was worth saving because even a small amount of food offers some sustenance.

Just like his dinner plate, Grandpa was the master of cleaning out jars and bottles of food and condiments as well. I could never clean out the jars enough to meet his satisfaction. He would always say, "Oh, you can get some more out of that," and then, he would proceed to take the knife and clean it out even further. To this day, I still feel ashamed when I "finish" a jar of food of which I know Grandpa would have been able to scrape out at least one more serving. He would clean out peanut butter and mayonnaise jars so meticulously that you would have thought the dog licked it clean. In fact, one of Grandpa's go-to sandwiches was peanut butter and mayonnaise, and I am convinced that he first made the sandwich because both jars were nearing empty. Rather than throwing them away or putting almost empty jars back in the cupboard, he figured he would just make a sandwich with what was remaining, and somehow, he actually grew to enjoy this odd combo. I know it probably sounds disgusting, and I'm sure most people would never think of putting that combination in a sandwich, but he was willing to try just about anything if it meant limiting even a small amount of waste. Many of my family members have shared that they, too, have adopted the practice of meticulously cleaning out jars, some even taking it a step further. My Aunt Stacey revealed that she even goes so far as to cut open the tube of toothpaste and scrape the sides of it to get every last bit. I know it sounds crazy, but you would be surprised how much longer a bottle of lotion or container of soap can last if you simply put in a little extra effort.

As much as Grandma and Grandpa tried to limit waste, though, you always had to be careful when getting things out of the refrigerator or pantry because you never knew what the expiration date might be. However, the expiration date never really mattered to my grandparents. As long as the food didn't smell spoiled, and there wasn't anything growing on it, they considered it edible. Even then, Grandpa was known to simply scrape the mold off the top and eat the unblemished parts, unphased by the fact that it was old enough to have fungi growing on it. I'm not sure if he ever got sick after doing this, but if he did, it wasn't enough to stop him from doing it again.

I remember visiting Grandpa one weekend after Grandma had passed. He had bought some soup from the church youth group that morning for us to eat for lunch, and as we were setting the table, he mentioned that he probably had some crackers to go with the soup. Sure enough, he found some buried in the back of the cupboard. He noted that the expiration date was from 2011, but after sampling a few, he said they were still good. Mind you, it was now the year 2020, yet he proceeded to eat the crackers, and as far as I could tell, enjoyed them at that. Needless to say, I ate my soup without crackers that day.

Grandpa's clothes are another example of how he limited waste. For one, he very rarely bought new clothes for himself as he didn't feel the need to fill his closet with items that he wouldn't wear regularly. Furthermore, he would wear his clothes until they were so worn that they had begun to fray at the hems and develop holes. Even then, he wouldn't get rid of them; rather, since Grandma had been a pretty good seamstress, he usually just had her patch them up and to him, they were good as new. He even asked my mom to sew his underwear for him once - he said there was no reason to buy something new when it could simply be fixed with a couple stitches. Now, if his clothing did reach a point where he was finally willing to admit they were no longer salvageable, he still wouldn't throw them away. Instead, he would use them as rags in his workshop or give the old jeans to Grandma so she had scraps to patch his jeans again in the future. He literally did not waste anything.

As you can tell, I admired Grandpa and the way he lived his life for many reasons, but this aspect of his life is something that I have grown to appreciate more and more. When you sit back and think about it, there is an alarming amount of waste in this world. Consider the amount of food a restaurant is expected to throw out at the end of the night per regulations - food that many around the world facing starvation or food insecurity would be incredibly grateful for. I used to work at a sporting goods store and as we would unpack new inventory, we would fill trash bags with the plastic and tissue paper in which each product had been individually wrapped. I remember questioning why so much packaging was necessary when it was basically going straight to a landfill. Even just driving through my neighborhood on trash pick-up days, it is sometimes upsetting to see how much waste can accumulate in just one week.

Let's face it - there is only one Earth, so we need to take care of it; otherwise, we will destroy it, and in turn, endanger humankind. Nature is a remarkable thing that ultimately sustains us, providing us with oxygen to breathe, nutritious foods to eat, and water to keep us hydrated. The environment is good to us, so we need to do our part and return the favor. Although I think it is most critical that change occur at the systemic level through new policies and legislation that hold people accountable, I recognize that most of us don't have the power to influence this level of reform. However, we do have the capacity to reduce our own carbon footprint by recycling, reusing, and simply being mindful of our impact on the environment. Now, I'm not saying that you need to go so far as to reuse your napkins, pick through the trash to salvage recyclables, or scrape mold off your food, but I do believe that we can all take steps to help preserve our planet.

Grandpa was so mindful of his impact on the environment, not only because of his appreciation for nature and understanding of its vital role in our existence, but he also recognized that his actions, no matter how small, could help preserve it. Even more so, though, I believe Grandpa wanted to do his part in protecting and saving the planet for future generations. He was thankful for his time here on Earth, and he wanted others, even those who are not born yet, to have the opportunity to enjoy the beauty of nature as well. Although some of his means may seem slightly unconventional, in his mind, he was just doing all he could to help maintain this beautiful planet, not only for him but for every living thing.

Life Lesson #4:

If we want to preserve our planet and the life it sustains, we must be mindful of our impact on the environment and do all we can to maintain it. Every act, no matter how small, matters.

Rule #5
If It's Broken, Fix It

One Christmas, Grandpa was given a sweatshirt with the phrase "Mr. Fix It" embroidered across the chest, and I remember thinking it was the perfect gift for him because I don't think he ever considered anything to be broken beyond repair. He would fix things that most people would simply throw away and replace with a new one. Shattered plates, tangled necklaces, chairs that were falling apart - in his mind, anything could be fixed with some glue or duct tape and a little bit of love.

Throughout my grandparents' house, you could find any number of plates, bowls, vases, and home decor that had been glued back together at one point or another, sometimes multiple times. Even the stained glass lamp that hovered above the kitchen table bore scars that had been mended with glue. It was actually pretty impressive how well Grandpa could take something that had been broken into pieces and make it whole again. Even those that had shattered into tiny little pieces, he would patiently gather every last one and then, carefully glue each intricate fragment back together. At a quick glance, most wouldn't even notice anything wrong with these objects, and more importantly, they always worked just as well as they had before. I do recognize that this requires time, patience, and a certain amount of skill, but this was just another way Grandpa liked to cut down on waste.

Many things around the house had been repaired with duct tape as well - tools for the garden, lawn chairs on the back porch, and the grandkids' hockey sticks to name a few. Just as with broken glass, Grandpa didn't feel the need to throw these things away or replace them when they could easily be made almost good-as-new again. Now don't get me wrong, at a certain point, he would recognize that something may no longer be useful, but if this was the case, he would still try to salvage every last piece, either recycling it or putting it to use in another way.

Nowadays, we certainly live in a generation of abundance where anything you need is only a few clicks away, and the value placed on materialistic things and outward appearance further encourage us to throw away those that aren't perfect. However, Grandpa came from a generation that fixed things when they were broken rather than getting rid of them. Yes, it may be easier and more convenient to just buy a new one that will look much nicer, but I think there is a lot of value in taking the time to try to restore something that has been broken. In fact, I think there is a lot of beauty and character in the flaws of something that has been glued back together. Those flaws make that piece unique, and although it has scars, it is still more than capable of performing its job.

This idea does not simply pertain to broken household items though. I believe that this rule can be applied to people and relationships as well. Let's be honest, nobody is perfect. We all have our flaws, insecurities, and personal problems that more often than not, eventually come to light in the relationships we hold. Unfortunately, though, when faults do surface, we are sometimes quick to throw away those connections that at one time had been so precious to us. We see these flaws as weaknesses and dwell on how they burden us rather than doing our part to help heal the wounds of others by showing them kindness and compassion. Even the bond of marriage no longer seems sacred as the rates of divorce in this country are higher than ever. Rather than putting in the effort to fix problems, we choose to take the easier road and simply end things.

Even my grandparents' marriage was not perfect. I remember a time when I was worried that they were going to get a divorce because it seemed as if they were always bickering about something. As a young kid, I thought that fighting meant that couples didn't love one another anymore and that divorce was the only way out. However, my naive mind underestimated the power of love and the will to mend things that aren't working. Despite my grandmother's stubbornness, Grandpa would always do what needed to be done in order to make their marriage work. He recognized that the love he had for her far outweighed his need to be right.

Let's face it - relationships can be challenging. Trying to balance the needs and wants of two people isn't always easy, but if that relationship is founded on love, then I believe it's worth fighting for. When troubles arise, it is important to remember the love that you share with one another and find a way to make it work even if it does require a significant amount of time, patience, and compromise. It involves listening to one another, respecting the other's views, and sacrificing things for the sake of the relationship. It often requires setting one's pride aside to make sure that both people in the relationship feel valued, respected, and loved. In doing so, though, I believe you will come to cherish the relationship that much more because you've put in the extra time and effort to make it work. Again, it may not be easy, but I think that in the end, you will find that it was well worth it.

When Grandpa would fix things, it would take a lot of time and patience, but he never let that deter him. Rather, it was his commitment to maintaining his principles that fueled him. Not only did he want to limit waste, but even more so, he recognized the value in everything regardless of any imperfections. Just like those pieces of glass or ceramic that he would carefully glue back together, he knew that everything, especially people and relationships, could be fixed if you simply put in the time, effort, and most importantly, love. A broken plate can be glued back together and a leaky hose can be fixed with some duct tape, and although they may never be good-as-new, they still have value and purpose. As for people and relationships, again, nobody is perfect. We all have our flaws or some kind of baggage that we are carrying around. Whether it's a broken heart, a mental illness, or trauma from the past, though, I truly believe that anything can be healed with some kindness, compassion, and love. Although we may never be made whole again after those experiences, we can heal from them, and in my opinion, the scars that remain are beautiful because they represent how strong the love is of the person who took the time to care for those wounds. Sometimes, it may be the love that you have for yourself that allows you to heal, but I believe this is the most precious love of all.

So when flaws do come to light, don't be so quick to give up on that person. Instead, love them because that might be exactly what they need in order to heal. Broken pieces can be mended and things can be made whole again if we simply put forth the effort. So when something is broken or an imperfection appears, don't throw it away. Instead, fix it because a little time and love can go a long way.

Life Lesson #5:

If it's broken, fix it. It's as simple as that.

Rule #6
Smile

Grandpa had a smile that would light up a room. Now, I'm not going to lie, I wouldn't say he smiled a lot, but when he did, it was truly infectious. Whether he was enjoying a moment surrounded by family, laughing at a smartass comment made by one of his grandkids, or beaming with pride as he watched them from the sidelines, his joy was palpable. The greatest smile though, always appeared whenever he was holding a little baby girl; the way his eyes sparkled in those moments was absolutely priceless.

Now, I share this rule for a couple reasons. First and foremost, because I believe we need to find joy in every day. In a world that is seemingly filled with hatred, violence, and suffering, it is easy to get caught up in the negative and focus on the bad. However, on any given day, I feel there is always something to smile about. It may be something as simple as the sun shining or the laughter of a child, but in my opinion, those are beautiful things that can bring a little joy into our lives if we simply take the time to appreciate them. Let's face it - if you aren't able to enjoy life, then you will be miserable, and this life will surely weigh you down. Yes, some days it is easier to find that joy than others, but again, I truly believe there is always something to smile about. Just the fact that you are alive is something to be grateful for, so even on those days when it feels as though nothing is going your way, take a moment and ask yourself, "What made me smile today?" If your answer is "nothing," then take a few minutes to do something you enjoy because everyone deserves to find happiness in each and every day.

Secondly, I believe this rule is of value because there are actually health benefits associated with smiling, not only for you but for the recipient of the smile as well. When you smile, it releases chemicals in your brain - chemicals that improve mood, reduce stress, relieve pain, and even boost your immune system. And for those at whom the smile is directed, it can boost their mood and self-esteem as well. A smile doesn't just bring joy to those experiencing it - it can improve their well-being and potentially even lead to a longer life. It's an easy way to spread a little cheer while, at the same time, boost your own health as well as the wellness of others.

The main reason I share this rule, though, is because of the effect a simple facial expression can have on others. In my opinion, a genuine smile is one of the easiest ways to spread a little love in this world, something that I feel is desperately needed. Whether it is a stranger you are passing on the sidewalk or someone you have known for years, a smile can brighten a person's day and show them a little kindness. In my experience, a smile even has the power to turn one's day around. For example, when someone feels as though they are invisible or as if no one cares about them, a simple smile and genuine

"How are you?" could potentially be the kindness and encouragement that person needs in that very moment. Even a simple compliment has the power to let someone know they are seen and valued. You may never know the extent to which a small act of kindness can impact another, but I can say for certain, it will most definitely be a positive one.

Not only could Grandpa's smile make your worst day feel like your best, but it also had the power to make you feel special. Grandpa had a knack for making you feel as though you were the most important person in the room, and I truly believe that was always his intention. He wanted everyone to feel loved and valued which he achieved through his smile, but also through his kind, simple words, a sweet note in a birthday card, or a quick wink meant just for you. Grandpa had mastered the art of making everyone feel special, and he did so through simple yet meaningful gestures.

At the beginning of the coronavirus pandemic, I had made it a point to call Grandpa regularly because I couldn't even imagine how lonely he must have been in that big house all by himself. They weren't long conversations, usually lasting only 20 minutes or so, but they meant a lot to me, and I think he really appreciated them as well. One of these phone calls, in particular, meant the world to me because as we were ending the conversation, I remember Grandpa taking a long pause before finally saying, "Oh Alli, I love you so, so, so much," and I don't think I've ever felt more loved than in that moment. It was just a few simple words, but it was in the way he said them that I could feel the depth and the power of his love for me. I can still hear him saying these words as if I had just spoken with him yesterday, and I know I will hold this sentiment near and dear to my heart forever, but this is just one of the many moments in which he made me feel so special.

Again, my heart ached for Grandpa during the pandemic, so in addition to the phone calls, I had ordered a couple books to be shipped to his house as well. He didn't have a computer, therefore, no access to online shopping so I figured he could use a few new books to pass the time. In one of our weekly phone conversations, he mentioned that he read through the first book pretty quickly. He said that he really enjoyed it and told me he would let me borrow it because he thought I would enjoy it as well. Unfortunately, I did not get the opportunity to read it while he was alive, but when I did eventually open the book, I found several 4-leaf clovers tucked away in the pages, left there for me to find. Now, Grandpa had a knack for finding 4-leaf clovers. In fact, we found about forty of them, dried and pressed, lying on the table in Pop's room after he passed, and as my mom and Aunt Stacey were cleaning out the house, they discovered even more, coming across a box that was filled with a few hundred of them, all dried and pressed for safe keeping. Needless to say, he had an abundance of 4-leaf clovers, but the idea that he had placed some in a book specially for me brought a smile to my face.

As you can tell, Grandpa never needed to do anything extravagant for you to know how much he loved you. Although simple, his words and actions were always heartfelt and genuine, which in my opinion, is so much more meaningful than if he had bought an expensive gift. It wasn't just on birthdays or holidays, either, that he showered you with these thoughtful gestures, which again, makes them even more special because they were unexpected. So often we wait for special occasions - birthdays, anniversaries, momentous events - to celebrate others, but the truth is, we should be grateful for the people in our lives every day and show them how much we appreciate them regularly. It can be as simple as sending a quick text message to let them know you're thinking of them or buying an extra cup of coffee on your way to work just for them. You'd be amazed how powerful these simple acts of kindness can be and how much of a difference they can make in someone's day.

One day, I was scrolling through Instagram when I came across the account @dearstranger143. After viewing a few of their posts, I was immediately uplifted and inspired by the message they were sharing. The creators of the account were using the platform to share how they spread a little love in this world which they do so by handing out notes of encouragement, often tucked in a bouquet of flowers, to unsuspecting strangers. As they record these interactions from a distance, they are able to capture the sweet and genuine reactions of the recipients, and as I watch these video clips, it is truly heartwarming to see the pure joy these simple gifts elicit. I have not seen one of their posts in a while, but I hope they are still out there, encouraging others through these simple acts of kindness and inspiring others to do the same.

My dad is another person who has inspired me when it comes to these random acts of kindness. Just like Grandpa, I've always known my dad is a great man and have admired and respected all that he does for our family. However, my appreciation for him grew even more one evening when I went out to dinner with my parents. As we were finishing up our meal, my dad excused himself to go to the bathroom, but on his way back to our table, I noticed that he took a little detour to the waitress' stand. When I asked my mom what he was doing, she said he was probably paying for another table's bill. She said that he does this pretty often which is remarkable in and of itself, but the idea that he does this regardless of the fact that more often than not, he doesn't get to see the reaction of those individuals is even more honorable. His random acts of kindness are truly genuine and meant for the recipient; he may not receive any recognition or thanks for his generosity, but I'm sure he gets all the satisfaction he needs in knowing that he is spreading a little joy in this world.

The truth is, everyone has the power to have a positive impact in this world. Although it may seem as though we need fame or wealth to make a difference, it's important to remember that it is not just sizable contributions that create change. Consider a small pebble that is thrown into the middle of a lake. At first, it causes small ripples around it, and then, those small ripples lead to larger and larger ones, and eventually, those ripples will reach the shore. The same idea is true of small acts of kindness. A thoughtful gesture, something as simple as a smile or a sincere compliment, can brighten someone's day, and potentially, produce the "pay it forward" effect, enlightening them to do the same for others. You may never know how far your small acts of kindness may reach, but the possibilities are endless. Therefore, I challenge you to be that "pebble" every chance you get and shine your light because you have the capacity to change the world for the better.

I have always marveled at the power of a simple smile. You can never truly know what someone is going through in their life, but whether they are at a high point or a low point, I assure you that a genuine smile or other type of thoughtful gesture will always make one's day a little brighter. You don't need riches or fame or what this world defines as beauty to make a difference. It's gestures and gifts that come from the heart, not the wallet, that will leave a lasting impression. Just like small ripples create larger ones, a simple act of kindness can go a long way.

Life Lesson #6:

Smile because you have the power to make this world
a better place.

Rule #7
Talk Less, Listen More

One sentiment that was shared by many was that Grandpa was a man of few words, and I don't think this statement has ever been truer of another person. Grandpa very rarely had much to say regardless of the topic or the situation, and even his jokes were often just quick-witted one-liners. He always seemed content to simply sit back and take in a conversation rather than take part in it. Even when he was having a one-on-one conversation, he was always much more interested in hearing what the other person had to say rather than talking about himself or voicing his own thoughts. Reflecting on it now, he really only ever spoke much when he was asked a question.

I'm sure we can all think of somebody who seems to have an opinion about everything or always needs to add their "two cents" to every conversation. They are too busy trying to insert themselves into the dialogue that they aren't listening to what anybody else has to say. I don't mean to offend anyone, but truthfully, I tend to take the words of these types of people with a grain of salt because it often feels as if they are just "blowing smoke" again. It is difficult for me to respect the opinion of someone who is unwilling to consider the thoughts of anyone else. Like George Clooney once said, "You never really learn much from hearing yourself speak."

Don't get me wrong, we are all entitled to our own opinions and ideas, and we have the right to express them; however, I believe it is just as important to listen to what the other person has to say. And this doesn't simply mean being quiet so the other person can talk - it means listening in a way that lets that person know they are heard through eye contact and expressing genuine interest. Grandpa did this without fail. He was never one to push his opinions on others; rather, he was always more inclined to listen to what others had to share, recognizing that taking their thoughts into consideration would only make his own opinions and ideas more well-rounded.

Let's be honest, nobody has all of the answers; otherwise, there wouldn't be any poverty, chronic disease, mental illness, or other forms of suffering in this world. I truly believe there is something to be learned from all those with whom we come in contact if we simply keep an open mind. Even if they are younger, less educated, or come from a lower socioeconomic class, they have had different life experiences that have shaped their worldview and outlook, and by simply listening to them, we can gain a new perspective that we had maybe never considered before. Now, the thing that you learn might be that you want to avoid getting caught up in a conversation with that particular person in the future, but that is technically still a lesson learned, and at least you gave them a chance rather than just writing them off.

I think you would be amazed at what you can learn

when you simply take the time to listen to another person, especially when their background is different from your own. It could potentially give you a different perspective on things and maybe even allow you to see other people in a new light. I know that I am truly grateful for those people who have challenged my ways of thinking and have helped me consider another point of view because ultimately, it has allowed me to respect and appreciate people that much more.

Grandpa certainly was a quiet man, but I think this is what allowed his words, despite being few and far between, to be even more meaningful and have an even greater impact on those who heard them. When he spoke, you knew the matter was important to him as he had felt the need to voice his thoughts. It was actually pretty impressive how he could silence a room when he spoke up because everyone respected his thoughts and wanted to hear what he had to say. People wanted to gain whatever wisdom he was willing to share.

I remember a time shortly after Grandma had passed away when Grandpa encountered a husband and wife arguing. Typically, he would have simply minded his own business, but in this instance, he couldn't ignore it. He had just lost the love of his life, and I could tell how deeply it hurt him to see a married couple bickering over trivial matters. He didn't yell at them or take sides with either of them, but rather, he calmly asked them to respect and appreciate one another, reminding them that love is to be cherished and should never be taken for granted. They immediately fell silent as they recognized the power of his words. However, I believe it wasn't just the words he shared that got through to them, but it was also the way in which he spoke them. When he addressed the couple, he did not do it in a judgmental or condescending manner; rather, it was evident that he simply wanted to help.

When Grandpa spoke, there was always a lot of wisdom, value, and purpose in his words; however, I believe it was the way in which he conversed with others that allowed his message to really resonate with them. For one, he always weighed his words carefully, considering his audience and how they might react. Furthermore, his words were never intended to offend others or belittle them but rather, to build them up and encourage them. He was always respectful because he recognized that people are much more receptive to a message when it is shared with genuine love and concern instead of judgment and aggression.

I believe the main reason that Grandpa's words were so powerful, though, is because his words were always demonstrated in his actions. He didn't just "talk the talk," he also "walked the walk." I think oftentimes, when we consider individuals who have been at the forefront of meaningful change, we think of people who are very outspoken and vocal about their cause which is necessary to raise awareness and gain support. However, I have found that words are meaningless if they are not backed by action. For example, how often have politicians or other leaders vowed certain things to try to gain our support, but in the end, never follow through on those promises? How often do people say something simply because they know that's what the other person wants to hear even if they don't truly mean it? In my opinion, if you really want people to respect your thoughts and see the value in your words, your actions should always be a reflection of your speech.

These "rules" that I am sharing with you are not based on words that Grandpa had spoken over the years - in fact, he never *told* us how to live our lives at all. Rather, he led by example and showed us how to live because the truth is, there really is greater power in action than in words. He was a man of incredible integrity who would always do the right thing even if it wasn't the easiest thing to do. Grandpa didn't need to voice his opinions because he made sure that his life was always a reflection of the values he held, one of those being to listen to others because no matter how much you think you know, there is always more to learn.

I'm so grateful that Grandpa taught me to listen, and not just with my ears, but with my eyes and heart as well because there is much more to a conversation than just words. There is a lot that I have yet to learn, but I do know that my willingness to listen and observe will take me a lot further than my capacity to talk about my own opinions and ideas ever will. Furthermore, he taught me that when I do feel the need to get my point across, I shouldn't just "talk the talk"; I have to "walk the walk" as well because actions always speak louder than words.

Life Lesson #7:

Remember - no one has all of the answers. In order

for you to grow as a person as well as gain the respect of others, you need to be willing to listen.

Rule #8
Stay Humble

As I reflect on Grandpa's life, I do regret that I didn't ask more questions and inquire more about his life when I had had the chance. Even if I had, though, I doubt he would have divulged much anyway. In addition to being a man of few words, Grandpa was also an incredibly humble man, so he didn't like to talk about himself or the things he did. In my eyes, he had a lot to be proud of and many things he could easily brag about, but he was never one to seek the spotlight or praise for his efforts. He was just a selfless man who wanted to do good for others, not expecting anything in return. Rather, as the pastor shared at the memorial service, Grandpa recognized that he was simply blessed to be a blessing.

As I mentioned before, I believe that Grandpa's steadfast faith had a significant influence on the way he lived his life, and this rule is no exception. He considered everything he had to be a gift from God, from basic necessities such as food and water to luxuries and everything in between. For this reason, he never bragged about what he had or did; rather, he was simply grateful and wanted to share those blessings.

Grandpa was always helping others, but he very

rarely spoke about it, so I'm sure there are many good deeds we aren't even aware of. In fact, it wasn't until after he passed away that I finally learned of some of his most admirable acts including the time he saved both his father and mother-in-law from a house fire. I don't know many details about this story, but I do know that he ran into the fire to pull them out, and I can't think of a more selfless act than this - to put one's own life at risk in order to save another. In my mind, that was certainly a moment to be proud of and something that I bet a lot of people would brag about for years to come, but he never mentioned it in all the times I was around him. Praise and commendation were never his motivation, but rather, his love for others is what fueled his selflessness.

Another example of both his generous heart and humility was revealed to us a day or two after he had passed, when a visitor dropped by the house to share his condolences. The man introduced himself and explained that he attended the same church as Grandpa. He said that although we probably didn't know who he was, he had felt compelled to share with us his personal experience as the recipient of Grandpa's kindness. As he proceeded to tell his story, he was overwhelmed with emotion, and we could all feel how deeply Grandpa's goodwill and generosity had impacted him. The man explained that earlier that year, the church had been organizing a mission trip to Puerto Rico, and he desperately wanted for his family to go, but unfortunately, they just couldn't afford it at the time. After hearing of this, though, Grandpa immediately offered to pay for the trip and not as a loan but as a gift. I'm sure Grandpa appreciated the man's desire to serve others and to teach his children to do the same, so I imagine Grandpa was grateful for the opportunity to help. However, we probably would have never known about this specific example of Grandpa's generosity if this individual had not taken the time to share his story with us. I think we can all agree that this was an incredibly generous and admirable act, but Grandpa certainly did not go around advertising his good deed or seeking the praise of others because that was just the type of man he was. When Grandpa did things for others, it came from the heart and was done out of love for humankind. They were genuine acts meant to build others up rather than himself. Furthermore, he never expected anything in return for his good deeds, nor did he feel the need to boast about them because again, he believed that the praise belonged to God, the true giver of every gift.

I always appreciate when people are willing to go out of their way for others, but in my opinion, those acts aren't so genuine when the people performing them are doing so in order to boost their own ego. Don't get me wrong, helping others is always a good thing, but when someone goes around bragging about it, it makes that act seem selfish. It's also disappointing when people start talking poorly about those they've helped, speaking about others' struggles when it's not their business to share. I don't know about you, but personally, I wouldn't want someone using my misfortune as a platform for their own gain and glory.

Helping others is certainly something to be proud of because there are many people who aren't willing to make those same sacrifices for others. Now, I understand that it is nice and encouraging to receive commendation for the good work you do, but I don't think it is necessary to go around seeking that praise. I know it can sometimes be disheartening when you feel as though your work is being taken for granted, but please do not lose hope or give up on your mission. Recognize that you are a blessing to those you serve, and although you may not receive immediate feedback, rest assured that you are making this world a better place. The acknowledgements will come, and you will be rewarded because I truly believe that what you put out in the world will come back to you one hundredfold. Furthermore, in my experience, recognition of your good works feels so much more genuine and meaningful when you aren't the one initiating it.

We have all been blessed with special traits and skills that make us unique, but I don't believe these attributes were intended for selfish purposes. Consider how fortunate you are because there are many people around the world who do not have the same financial, physical, or even emotional resources to serve others in the ways you are able. Therefore, be grateful for all that you have been given and use those gifts to spread good in this world because I believe that when we humbly offer our blessings to others, they will multiply and achieve so much more than we could ever imagine.

Life Lesson #8:

Always remain humble because ultimately, the gifts

that we are given can be taken away in the blink of an eye. Rather than boasting, be grateful and remember that you are blessed to be a blessing.

Rule #9
Be Patient - Good Things Take Time

Grandpa had the patience of a saint, and this was demonstrated in just about everything he ever did. Whether he was carefully constructing his latest wooden creation, intricately gluing broken pieces of ceramic back together, or caring for Grandma, he did everything with incredible poise. Grandpa never rushed through anything, nor did he become impatient when things weren't going his way. Just like a fine wine, he recognized that good things take time and that the best things in life don't simply happen overnight. Furthermore, he lived with the mentality that if it's something you really care about, you'll take the extra time with it because the greater the effort, the better the results.

Grandpa was an expert craftsman who constructed many beautiful pieces of woodwork over the years, from cradles and child-sized dining sets to kitchen bars and bedroom furniture. I was always impressed with how detailed his creations were, using beveled edges and carving intricate designs into the wood rather than simply using basic shapes and right angles. No offense to IKEA, but I would much rather furnish my home with the pieces Grandpa made as not only were they unique with many complex details, but I also know how much time and love were put into them. Grandpa took pride in his work, so rather than rushing through a project just to get it done, he would go over every little feature, fine-tuning it until it met his satisfaction.

His patience, fine craftsmanship, and attention to detail were visible in the way he restored the family's farmhouse as well. Every time I walk through their house, I am amazed at how elaborate the rooms are, and I can only imagine the countless hours he spent designing and perfecting every intricate detail. From the wallpaper he hung with expert precision to the bricks he laid in perfect patterns, it was evident that he put a lot of time and effort into this particular project. His creativity was demonstrated in the character of the house as well from the exposed wooden beams and built-in bookcase in the living room to the cozy window seat situated next to a fireplace in the corner of the dining room. Grandma's sewing table, the deep window sill in the kitchen for her to display her many trinkets, the large dining room for family gatherings, and the screened-in back porch where they would spend many of their summer nights - Grandpa clearly designed the house with his family and their interests in mind.

Although Grandma was probably nagging him to finish the house, I doubt this made him work much faster as he probably considered this to be the most important project he would ever complete. Grandpa put a lot of love and care into everything he did, but for the home that meant so much to Grandma and the place where his own family would reside, I'm sure this love and care were a hundredfold.

Grandpa had many other unique skills that required

a great deal of care and patience as well such as tying perfect bows and getting knots out of necklaces. Even the way he carved the Thanksgiving turkey and arranged the pieces on the platter was impressive. I didn't realize it until the first Thanksgiving after he had passed away when my dad took on this responsibility. I know he tried his best, but if I'm being honest, he kind of butchered it.

Some people may consider this extra effort a waste of time, but I know that to Grandpa, it was always worth it because not only did he take pride in his work, but he knew how pleased others would be with the end result as well. One of Grandma's most prized possessions was her set of fine china that Grandpa had purchased for her while he was stationed in Japan. The set included at least fifty pieces from dinner plates and bowls to serving dishes and a tea set, all of which he shipped to her from halfway around the world. Mind you, this was the 1950's, so I imagine the ride was not nearly as smooth as it would be nowadays. Miraculously, though, every last piece arrived whole and without blemish, but I'm not surprised by this. I can picture Grandpa individually wrapping each piece of china in layers of bubble wrap and newspaper and packing them securely into boxes. I've thought about how much easier it would have been for him to find some local china when he returned to the States - something that he could simply drive home from the store. However, I imagine that when he saw this particular set, he knew how much Grandma would love it and in my opinion, the fact that he sent it all the way from Japan, makes the gift even more meaningful.

Grandpa did everything thoughtfully and carefully, from the words he spoke to his craftsmanship and even the way he performed simple, daily tasks. For example, I think that after most people have emptied a plastic grocery bag, they either throw it away or if they save it, they shove it into another plastic bag that is already overflowing with them. Grandpa, though, would always fold them up nicely and add them to the organized pile of bags he kept in the cupboard to be reused in the future. From meticulously cleaning out peanut butter jars to the way he would glue those intricate pieces of ceramic back together, he did everything with incredible patience regardless of how menial the task might be.

I think we all put a little extra time and effort into things that mean the most to us. To Grandpa, though, everything mattered, so he always gave his best, recognizing that a greater effort always leads to a better outcome. And not only was this true of the way he constructed things and performed daily tasks, but he maintained this philosophy when it came to people and relationships as well.

Grandpa's patience was always evident, but it was especially noticeable in the way he cared for Grandma, particularly in the later years of their marriage. Now, I loved my grandmother very much, but if I'm being completely honest, she was a bit of a spitfire and as stubborn as they come. She did not have the patience of a saint and was always quick to share her gripes. Growing up, I remember many of those complaints being directed at Grandpa, and although he had an incredible amount of patience, Grandma always seemed to know how to press his buttons. Understandably, he would feel the need to share his point of view, but this never swayed Grandma whatsoever, so they would bicker back and forth for a little while before Grandpa would finally walk away because he knew his efforts were futile. In the end, though, he would always do whatever needed to be done in order to make Grandma happy, regardless of how misguided her complaints may have been. He did his best to remain patient with her because he knew that overreacting and losing his temper would only make the situation worse. Being the "Mr. Fix It" that he was, Grandpa was always more concerned with finding a solution rather than being right; therefore, he allowed his love for her to guide his interactions rather than his pride.

Then, when Grandma was in her early 80's, the signs of dementia started to show. At first, it was a misplaced wallet, forgetting a word here and there, or sometimes she would ask the same question several times within the span of a few minutes. Next, it was her cooking as we started to notice that things just didn't taste quite as good as they used to. Although subtle, we knew something was wrong, and when we got the official diagnosis, we were devastated.

If you have ever been around someone with dementia, you know how horrible a disease it is and how difficult it is to watch someone slowly lose their ability to remember things. For Grandma, it was incredibly frustrating because especially early on, she knew she was forgetting things that should have been second nature to her. For Grandpa, though, this diagnosis was even more disheartening as not only was he there to witness her steady decline, but even more so, there was absolutely nothing he could do about it. The only thing he could do was care for her the best he could, and it was in the way that he took on this responsibility that his patience and selflessness shone through more than ever.

In the beginning, it was the doctor's appointments, organizing medications, managing her nutrition, fielding repetitive questions, and reminding her of people and things she couldn't recall. As she became sicker and the dementia began to deprive her of the little independence she had remaining, it was helping her walk from room to room, bathing her, and cleaning up after her when she couldn't make it to the bathroom in time. It was a full-time job, and although it was difficult and heartbreaking to witness her decline, he did all of these things with incredible patience and without complaint. The thought of placing her in a nursing home never even crossed his mind. He knew he was capable of caring for her, and he knew he would provide her with the best care because he did it with unconditional love. And even more so, he wanted to be by her side every moment he possibly could.

Just a few months before Grandma passed away, my sister was able to capture the sweetest picture of our grandparents holding hands during a short walk they had taken to get some exercise and fresh air for Grandma. Even more impressive, she was able to take the shot so that the two homes Grandpa had built and restored and in which they had raised their family together were visible in the background. That picture is now displayed in all of our homes as a reminder of the love they had shared and the love that continues to guide our family. As precious as the picture is, though, the story behind the moment makes it even more sentimental.

My Aunt Stacey and my sister had been visiting, so they suggested taking a walk to Grandma's "spot." There is a tree stump that sits at the edge of their property, no more than a hundred yards from the house, and when Grandma would go for a walk, she would always stop and sit on that stump to rest. On this particular day, she was doing just that - resting on her stump. But when it was time to go back to the house, she was being her usual stubborn self and refusing to get up.

After several failed attempts by my Aunt Stacey and sister, Grandpa very calmly reached out his hand and said in the sweetest voice, "Can I hold my little lady's hand?"

My sister said that Grandma's eyes lit up and the most innocent smile appeared, just like she was 17 again. How could she refuse such a kind offer? And as they strolled back to the house, hand in hand, it was a testament to their enduring love for one another - Grandma, in her dementia-altered mind, reverting back to a time when their love was young and just beginning to bloom, and Grandpa, reminiscing and full of gratitude for the many wonderful years they had shared.

I'm sure it was in moments like this that Grandpa found the strength and encouragement to continue caring for Grandma. It was difficult enough for me to watch the decline in her memory and health, so I can only imagine how devastating it was for Grandpa to observe it day in and day out. To put so much love and effort into someone who cannot reciprocate that care or even express their gratitude requires an extraordinary amount of patience and unconditional love, but he did it each and every day regardless of how defeated he felt. His love and patience are what made these bright moments possible, and although they may have been few and far between at times, it was the motivation he needed to keep going.

Granted, it is much easier to be patient with those whom we love and cherish, but it wasn't just with his wife or even his family that he demonstrated this type of patience. He was that way with everyone, which in my opinion, is a pretty remarkable trait. Let's be honest, people can be frustrating to work with sometimes, and it's very easy to become impatient with someone who is clearly not on the same page as you. I understand how difficult it can be to keep your cool when your child has still not put their toys away even though you've asked them to do so at least ten times. It is extremely annoying when an entitled customer feels the need to waste your time with an endless series of questions, especially when you have countless others you need to attend to as well. And I will be the first to admit that I become impatient with the driver in front of me who seems quite content to drive five miles per hour under the speed limit in a no passing zone. But what does losing our patience with these people accomplish? With your children, they may finally put those toys away, but they will probably be upset and you will more than likely feel a slight sense of guilt. If you lose your cool with that annoying customer, they may stop, or they may ask to speak to your manager and file a complaint against you. And for the slow driver, they may pull over and let you pass or your road rage could lead to an accident. Even if your impatience does get you what you want, though, the lack of respect shown toward the other person, honestly, just makes you seem like a jerk.

When it comes to being patient with others, I think a good rule of thumb is to put yourself in their shoes and rather than losing your temper with them, consider why they might be behaving in such a manner. Maybe that person who is driving so slowly has just left the hospital where they've received some bad news. Blaring the horn and yelling at them is definitely not what they need in that moment. Maybe the customer who is asking all those questions has just found out they are finally pregnant after trying for years, and she wants to make sure that she is buying the best products for her unborn child. Now, it very well might be that somebody is intentionally trying to get a rise out of you, but if that is the case, don't give them the satisfaction of losing your cool for their amusement or so they can get something that they want. If they choose to be petty, that's on them, but you can decide how you will respond, and in my opinion, being the bigger person is better than trying to argue your point with someone who is never going to admit they are wrong. I think that in some cases, simply walking away is the best thing we can do.

I think it's also important to remember that we are all human, and we all make mistakes. Whether or not we're willing to admit it, I'm sure we have all been in a situation where we recognize that we messed up, so in those moments, consider how you would want others to treat you. Negative criticism often lowers a person's self-esteem and confidence, most likely causing them to feel more anxiety in similar situations, and thus, more prone to make mistakes again. I believe that if you do need to address any flaws, constructive criticism will be much more effective, especially when you offer it with genuine care and concern. In my experience, people are much more receptive to feedback when they are not feeling attacked. I know it can be challenging to keep our cool sometimes, but I promise you that remaining patient in these situations will produce a much more positive outcome than losing your temper ever will.

Nowadays, we seem to live in an era of instant gratification. Unlike Grandpa and the people of his generation, we no longer rely on things such as encyclopedias, phone books, or store catalogs because now these things are all accessible through one small device that we carry with us everywhere. We can "Google" just about anything and have an answer within seconds, and cell phones allow us to communicate with others at all times of the day via text message, voice calling, social media, or email. Thanks to Amazon Prime, packages can now be delivered within a day or two, and there is no longer a need to wait in line when you can simply order ahead and have your food waiting for you when you arrive. Don't get me wrong, there are certainly benefits of technology, and I am grateful for many of the advancements that have been made, but unfortunately, I feel as though we are creating a society that no longer knows how to wait for anything. Think about it - how often do we get frustrated when we don't get an immediate response to a text message because we know that person is always on their phone? And even though our phones grant us access to just about anything we need within seconds, we can still become impatient when the Wi-Fi is just a little too slow.

I recognize that it can be difficult to remain patient in this fast-paced world, and I completely understand the desire for immediate gratification; I mean, who doesn't want fast money, instant success, or their dreams to be fulfilled overnight? But the truth is, many of the best things in life take time. Skill development, meaningful relationships, achieving a dream that you've worked so hard to accomplish - these things require significant time and patience. However, I think you will come to realize that more effort leads to better results, and hopefully, you will have an even greater appreciation for the outcome.

I know it can be discouraging when you feel as though your efforts do not seem to be producing the results you are hoping for, but don't give up. Remember, good things take time and the best things in life do not happen overnight, so if you aren't satisfied with where you are in life right now, don't lose faith. Instead, remain patient and continue to work hard because I believe putting in the extra time will always be worth it as ultimately, that dedication will generate even better results than you could have ever imagined.

Life Lesson #9:

Be patient - the best is yet to come.

Rule #10
Live Simply

A classic phrase that I have heard over the years is "it's not like back in the good ol' days," and to be honest, I've used the saying on occasion as well. I'm sure when most people use this phrase, though, they are referring to a time well before I was born, but I do believe there are certain things from each previous generation that people appreciate and wish would have survived the passage of time. For me, I have always appreciated the time when things were much simpler - the days before smartphones, social media, and self-driving cars, and when Sundays were truly a day of rest rather than another day to "get ahead." This was yet another quality of Grandpa's that I really respected and admired. Despite all of the advancements in technology, the transition to a faster-paced lifestyle, and many people's need to "keep up with the Joneses," he always seemed quite content to maintain the simpler lifestyle, just like back in the good ol' days.

Although Grandpa was around when technology was progressing at a rapid pace, he did not feel the need to buy into the hype. He never owned a computer, never had an email address, and the only reason he had a cell phone was because his children bought one for him so that he could take it with him on long bike rides in case of emergency. Even then, it was the most basic flip phone you could buy, and most of the time it was turned off and tucked away in the small corner desk in the kitchen. His clothes were simple as well, wearing a pair of worn-out blue jeans, a white undershirt, and one of his plaid button-downs almost every day. My grandparents very rarely bought anything new for themselves, they never took extravagant trips, and their ideal date night was dinner at Pizza Hut. For them, it was never about what they had or where they went - rather, it was always about who they were with. They didn't care about keeping up with the latest trends or eating fancy dinners at upscale restaurants. They didn't find happiness in things - they found joy in the presence of those they loved.

Unfortunately, we now live in a world that is hell-bent on stealing our happiness and contentment as these days, society seems to revolve around stuff and status. From materialism and money to technology and social media, society seems to be screaming, "More, more, more. You need more!" Think about it - Apple comes out with a new iPhone every year, and although they may make a few improvements, it's not all that different from the previous one. Yet, people are still lined up at stores on the day of its release, ready to buy it, even if the phone they already have works just fine. Furthermore, a lot of people now choose to lease their vehicles rather than buying them so they can always have the newest model, and we even fill our closets with current fashion trends that will ultimately go out of style within a year or two. It doesn't matter that we already have more than enough clothing - when the latest trend comes around, we have to have it.

I admit that I don't know a lot about economics and what it takes to establish a sustainable market. I do understand that consumers need to put money into the economy for it to thrive, but I think some corporations are taking advantage of this so that they can make more money for themselves. For one, it's almost as if products these days are intentionally made to break after a few years so that you're forced to buy a new one, the latest and greatest one at that. They used to build things to last, but now you're lucky if you can get ten good years out of an appliance or piece of equipment. Even more so, though, we are inundated with stuff on a daily basis. Everywhere we go, we see countless advertisements for the latest products, and even social media has been designed to promote the things that you've recently searched on your phone. Companies are continually developing new products, "get rich quick" schemes, and apps that they market as "must-have" commodities if you want to keep up with the times. These large corporations have built their businesses on extorting our desire for more and encouraging us to get what everyone else has. Furthermore, they manipulate us into thinking their products will improve our lives and make us happier, but the truth is, most of these companies don't care about our well-being; they only care about our money.

For some reason, it feels as though money is becoming more important than humanity in many aspects of our lives. Rather than creating an economy that looks out for the "little guy," inflation and the desire for wealth continue to drive the cost of living higher and higher to the point where it is incredibly difficult for low-income households to afford even basic necessities. Even if we don't want to admit it, we still rely on people to perform minimum-wage jobs, but how can we expect someone to do this line of work if they can't live off the income?

It's not just the large corporations that allow this to happen though; it seems as though everyone wants to be rich because again, that is what society says will make us happy. Even if we have enough to sustain us, we still want more. Consider those who are working in some of the most well-paid jobs - they are still looking for additional ways to boost their income, making work their priority because that is what will help them get ahead. Furthermore, society continues to push a lot of "get rich quick" schemes as well, whether it is gambling on just about anything, including the length of the National Anthem at the Super Bowl, or offering opportunities to earn fast money through apps and social media platforms. These fads draw people in because who doesn't want to make a quick buck, but are these companies really looking out for your best interest? They say that money can't buy happiness and although many people disagree with this statement, I believe it is true. Having money only makes us want more.

As for social media, I believe this is one of the greatest "thieves" of our happiness these days. Don't get me wrong, there are a lot of benefits to social media such as the ability to stay in touch with loved ones far away, keeping up on the latest news, and learning new things that are of interest to us. However, there are disadvantages that come with it as well. First, I think social media has caused people to develop a false sense of reality as most people are only posting the best aspects of their lives or making it appear as though everything is perfect. When we start to compare ourselves to only half of the picture, we become discouraged because we feel as though our lives are not nearly as fulfilling. Furthermore, social media has provided yet another platform for people to criticize and bully others, and the pressure of needing to post something as well as the disappointment that comes when you don't get enough "likes" can be incredibly disheartening for some. Finally, I believe the greatest downside to social media is that it is a distraction that takes away from real human connection and our ability to simply live in the moment. It honestly breaks my heart when I see a group of teens hanging out, but nobody is talking because they are all glued to their phones. It also saddens me when I see a child trying to get their mother's attention, but she is too busy scrolling through social media to give the child the attention he deserves. It feels like everywhere I go, I see people who are so absorbed in their phones that they can't appreciate all that is going on around them.

Today's society encourages us to accumulate more stuff, make more money, and "keep up with the Joneses" as a means of finding happiness, but I believe it is this type of lifestyle that is stealing our contentment. It causes us to spend so much time comparing ourselves to others, wanting what they have, or seeking their approval that we forget to appreciate everything that we already have.

Consider how lucky you are when there are millions of people around the world who don't even have access to basic necessities such as food and clean drinking water. We live in a country of abundance and most necessities are readily available if we have the means, but not everyone has this luxury. I have seen firsthand the challenges that those living in poverty endure on a daily basis; however, I have also witnessed the pure joy that they find in the simplest of things. To see the way a child's face lights up after receiving someone's old shirt and a pair of used soccer cleats is truly priceless. It makes me realize how blessed I am and how often I take simple things such as a new shirt for granted. Then, it makes me wonder, "Why do I accumulate so many unnecessary things when there are people around the world with so little? Why am I not content with all that I have, when they can find such joy in a second-hand shirt?"

Now, I'm not asking you to completely abandon your current lifestyle and never buy anything for yourself that you do not need because I do understand wanting to have nice things that make you happy. However, I am asking you to just stop and take a second to think before you impulsively purchase something. Ask yourself, "Why am I buying this?" If your answer is "I want to impress people," "I want to fit in," or "It would make a great social media post," I think you should reconsider. You need to do what makes *you* happy, not what you think will impress others or gain their approval.

It's okay to want - it's hard not to - but remember

to be grateful for what you do have and rather than relying on *things* to bring you happiness, consider the value of all the intangible things in this life such as meaningful relationships, memorable experiences, and time with loved ones - things that money can't buy.

I had a basketball coach in high school who would always talk about "the little things." He would preach about the importance of taking care of the ball, making smart decisions, and making our lay-ups because all of those little things are ultimately what win games. We would all kind of roll our eyes when he would say this because it felt like we were listening to a broken record, but the truth is, he was right, and not just about basketball, but he was right about life, too. Unfortunately, he stepped down as head coach before my senior season, but he was still there cheering us on as we made our run in the playoffs that year. At some point before the championship game, he had managed to slip a little note for my sister and me into our mailbox. In it, he wished us good luck, but also reminded us that basketball is such a small part of life - a little thing that can leave you with lasting memories. He ended his letter with these words: "Little memories last for years! Little dreams can lead to greatness, little victories to success. It's the little things in life!"

I think too often we lose sight of the significance that little moments hold, and don't always appreciate them for what they are because one day, it's the little things that we will look back on and miss the most. Rocking your baby to sleep, embracing loved ones in a hug, or just the ability to sit in their presence - in my opinion, these things have so much more value than anything money could buy. So please, don't let these moments pass you by because you were too busy scrolling through social media or sending work emails during family time. These moments are precious, and no amount of money or "likes" can ever replace them.

I have always marveled at the sheer joy a child can experience from the simplest of things - a game of peek-a-boo, an airplane flying overhead, or even playing in a cardboard box. I sometimes think, "When do we lose that sense of awe and wonder?" and better yet, "How can we maintain that ability to find joy in the little things?"

I think that in order to do this, we need to stop placing our self-worth in our money, possessions, and the number of "likes" we get on our Instagram posts. Instead, we need to recognize that our self-worth lies in our character, and I believe that once we realize this, we can begin to focus on what will ultimately allow us to find peace and contentment in this life - things that money can't buy.

Grandpa never needed much to find contentment, and he certainly never relied on things to bring him happiness. Furthermore, the things he owned were never for show as he didn't feel the need to impress others with what he had or seek their approval. Yet, people still respected and appreciated him because what I've learned is that if you have a good heart, people won't care what you're wearing or how much money you have. Unfortunately, there will probably always be a few haters and people who continue to judge, but my advice then, is to say a prayer for them because in my opinion, they have not yet figured out what is truly important in this life.

Don't spend your time here on Earth in pursuit of money, possessions, and the approval of others because those aren't the things that are going to bring you joy and a sense of fulfillment. Don't spend your days chasing more when you already have all that you need. It's those little things that make life worth living, so live simply and don't let this world steal your happiness.

Life Lesson #10

Live simply and be true to yourself because when you are set free from the need for stuff and status, it allows you to see the natural beauty in this world and enjoy the little things in life.

Rule #11
Family Comes First

Without a doubt, family was the absolute most important thing to Grandpa, and he always put us above and before all else no matter what the circumstances. In fact, everything he ever did was for his family. Whether it was working countless hours to provide financially, lovingly restoring not one but two houses so there would be a nice place to live, or traveling here, there, and everywhere to attend sporting events, school performances, and other family gatherings, he was always putting us first. I know he genuinely enjoyed these things and never viewed them as sacrifices, but as I reflect on Grandpa's dedication to his loved ones, I am reminded of how much he truly cherished the bond of family.

Grandpa was a family man first and foremost, and he went above and beyond to fulfill that role. He guided us, provided for us, supported us in any way he could, and showered us with unconditional love always. We never had to question if he would be there for us because he always was without fail.

As I attempt to share what I consider to be some of the most memorable stories and the moments that have left the greatest impression on me, I'm not sure my words will do any justice. Grandpa's dedication to our family was tangible, something that you would have had to experience firsthand in order to gain a true understanding of the depth and power of his love. However, I hope that in reading my words, you will at least come to appreciate your own family a little more and recognize that making time for them is so important because you never know when you will no longer have the opportunity to do so.

My family is spread throughout the country from Colorado and Texas to New York and New Hampshire, but fortunately, I grew up in much closer proximity to my grandparents. We lived just forty minutes away from them, which in central Pennsylvania is pretty close considering it takes about half an hour to get anywhere really. Growing up, my brother, sister, and I would spend a week or two with our grandparents during the summer as well as weekends throughout the year. We always enjoyed these visits which often included activities such as baking cookies, playing cards, bike rides with Grandpa, and chasing softballs at Uncle Scot's slow-pitch games. We were active kids to say the least, but our grandparents always kept us busy. I'm sure they were exhausted by the time we finally went home to our parents, but I know they enjoyed every minute just as much as we did.

As my siblings and I got older, we continued to keep them busy as all three of us were involved in sports year-round. Between school, club, and township teams, our family's schedule was jam-packed with sporting events, sometimes having games scheduled for six out of the seven days in a week. However, it didn't matter if the game was near or far, rain or shine, Grandma and Grandpa were at Every. Single. One. They were there for the all-day softball tournaments in the 90-degree heat and humidity. During soccer season, when it was freezing cold, you would still find them on the sidelines, although they were a little harder to spot because they were bundled up in layers of coats and blankets. At one point, my twin sister and I had three different games in three different locations on Saturdays, but the travel and long day were certainly not going to stop them from being there to cheer us on.

They were our biggest fans and most avid supporters. Grandpa would bring a small notebook and pencil with him to every game so that he could record our individual statistics including points, steals, assists, and he even kept track of our batting averages during softball season. As my mom and Aunt Stacey started cleaning out my grandparents' old farmhouse after their passing, they came across these notebooks as well as countless newspaper clippings and game programs. As I read through some of those old stat books and articles, I was reminded of how much their steadfast support meant to me over the years. Just knowing they were on the sidelines, motivated me even more because I wanted to make them proud.

I'm sure there are many grandparents who are always there, cheering on their grandchildren in the various activities in which they are involved. In fact, I was fortunate enough to have all four of my grandparents at the majority of my events over the years. However, I believe my grandparents went above and beyond in this area, just as they always did for family. Their schedules revolved around our sporting events, always making them a priority, and honestly, I don't think there was anything that would have stopped them from attending our games. Just let me share a few occasions, in particular, that I feel truly demonstrate their commitment and dedication.

The first game that comes to mind was a basketball game my senior year of high school. I remember our team going through our usual warm-up routine prior to the game during which I would always scan the stands to see where my family was sitting and who all had come to watch us play. This night, though, I did not see my grandparents, which was out of the ordinary for them, but I just assumed they were running a little late on this particular night. Shortly before the game was about to begin, I finally saw Grandma stroll in and join my family in the bleachers. However, Grandpa was nowhere to be seen. I then noticed my dad get up and walk out of the gym, only to return halfway through the second quarter with Grandpa in tow. I was relieved that they had both made it to the game, but definitely still curious as to why they had arrived late and separately.

After the game, though, I learned that my grandparents had been in a car accident on the way to the school. Their Toyota Camry had been totaled, but fortunately, they were unharmed, or so we assumed as they both refused medical attention. Grandma had actually hitched a ride to the game with a complete stranger while Grandpa had stayed behind to take care of the paperwork. And if my dad had not gone to check on him, I'm willing to bet Grandpa would have hitchhiked to the game as well.

There was another game during my freshman year of college in which my soccer team had made it to the third round of playoffs. It was mid-November and there was snow on the ground, but my grandparents still made the two-hour drive to watch me play, just as they always did. Despite the sub-freezing temperatures and the bitter wind blowing at their backs, they cheered me on throughout the long 90-minute game, continuing to display their support of my athletic career.

After losing a hard-fought battle that day, I went and visited briefly with my family before it was time to get back on the bus. Grandpa wrapped me in one of his special hugs and gave me a big smile, telling me how proud he was. In this moment, he had seemed his usual self, nothing out of the norm. Little did I know, he had been enduring much more than the frigid weather that day. Apparently he had been sitting through the match on those cold metal bleachers with kidney stones. Now, I have never had kidney stones, but I have heard from others that they cause excruciating pain; some say they are even worse than childbirth. However, Grandpa watched the entire game without mentioning the terrible pain that I can only imagine he was experiencing because then he may have had to leave. Like I said, I don't think there is anything that would have kept my grandparents from being there to cheer us on.

Grandpa's encouragement of his children's, grandchildren's, and even great-grandchildren's countless endeavors over the years was just one of the many ways in which he supported us. In my opinion, though, his selflessness was always the thing that stood out the most to me. Grandpa was incredibly generous, always putting the needs and wants of others before his own, and this was especially true when it came to his family as it was evident that the happiness and well-being of his family were always his primary concern.

I feel as though I've already shared so many examples of Grandpa's selflessness over the years, but it wasn't just the significant moments that demonstrate his kindness. It was all the little sacrifices he made as well. My Uncle Scot recalled how he would often ask Grandpa to throw baseball with him in the backyard in the evenings. Although this was typically after a long day of work for him and he probably had a hundred other things he needed to do, Grandpa would always agree. He never complained or used some excuse to get out of it. Instead, he simply embraced the moment, enjoying the opportunity to play baseball with his boy.

There was a time shortly after my grandmother had passed when my mom and I were visiting Grandpa. It was just about dinnertime, so he suggested we get Larry's which was their go-to spot for their favorite food, pizza. When he asked us what toppings we wanted on the pizza, we said we were good with pepperoni which was what he and Grandma had always ordered.

On this night, though, he said, "Oh, you want more than that, don't you?"

We ended up getting a pizza with the works - sausage, pepperoni, peppers, and onions - something my grandmother would have hated and most likely refused to eat. That's when it dawned on me. He had been eating pepperoni pizza all those years because that is what she had wanted. He never complained about it or asked for anything different, so as far as any of us knew, he had always just wanted pepperoni as well. It may not seem like much, but that is a long time to be putting your pizza preferences aside, and I'm willing to bet that there were many other meals in which Grandpa simply ended up eating whatever Grandma was in the mood for. I think Grandpa had figured out the whole "happy wife, happy life" thing pretty early on in their marriage.

Grandpa was always putting others before himself, but in my opinion, the stories that I have already shared pale in comparison to this next one. Like I mentioned previously, Grandpa never complained about anything, and any pain he ever experienced was no exception to this. If he did mention he was hurting, you knew it was serious, and this was one of those few occasions. On this particular day, my uncle had stopped by my grandparents' house on his way home from work to visit and check in with them. Shortly after he arrived, though, Grandpa admitted that he was having some pretty intense chest pain. My uncle immediately called 9-1-1 and requested an ambulance to take him to the hospital. Now, I'm guessing while most people wait for an ambulance to pick them up, their thoughts are mostly filled with worry about their own health, and understandably so. However, to my uncle's surprise, Grandpa used this time to organize Grandma's medications for the week. Even when he was experiencing life-threatening pain, he still was not thinking of himself. His greatest concern at that moment was wondering who was going to take care of his wife if he wasn't able to do so.

Grandma always said that she married Grandpa because of his red hair, but it probably helped that he spoiled her. Some may call him whipped or spineless, but that wasn't the case at all. Grandpa was wired differently, preferring to satisfy the needs of those he loved rather than his own. He was a giver who found so much more joy in making others happy, so in a sense, he was getting what he wanted as well. I'm sure there were moments where he may have felt a little discouraged, as though his needs and wants weren't being fulfilled, but if this was the case, he never expressed it, and it never seemed to weigh him down. Again, his priority was always his family and ensuring they were happy and taken care of.

The best thing about Grandpa's generosity and selflessness was that he never expected anything in return. However, if you did want to repay the favor, the greatest gift you could give him was your time.

Grandpa valued family time more than anything. He was never happier than when he was surrounded by his children and their families, and he fully embraced every second of those moments. I had always known that he treasured this time with family, but I remember one night, in particular, when this love became even more evident to me. We were wrapping up one of our traditional Christmas get-togethers, and those of us remaining were gathered around the dining room table playing Skip-Bo, our way to unwind after a hectic day of cooking, eating, opening gifts, and cleaning up. At this point, it was usually getting pretty late, but family means as much to my mom as it did to my grandparents so we always made it a point to spend a little extra time with them at the end of the night. We had already played one round, so it was safe to assume that my family would be leaving once round two ended. Grandpa, though, was bound to make that round last as long as possible.

From my position next to him, I could clearly see his hand. I swear I was not trying to cheat; he just wasn't doing a very good job of hiding his cards. Anyway, if you've ever played Skip-Bo before, you know that a "Skip-Bo" is essentially a wild card and can be played anywhere. Well, at this stage in the game, Grandpa only had two cards remaining in his stockpile (the pile you are trying to get rid of in order to win) and three Skip-Bo cards in his hand. He could have easily won the game, but instead, I watched as he simply added to his discard pile on each of his next three turns. Now, I am a competitive person, as is most of my family, so winning is always my focus when we play card games. Grandpa, on the other hand, recognized that him winning the game would have ended the night and the valuable family time that he cherished. He clearly wanted to savor as much of that moment as he possibly could.

Grandpa was always intentional about spending time with family. It wasn't just with his wife and children, though. I always appreciated how he would continue to make time for his mother as well. Although he was one of eight children, he was always the one who included her in everything, picking her up for family gatherings and dropping her off afterwards. She would spend many of the holidays with our family as well, and when we would spend Saturdays together making applesauce, strawberry jelly, or baking cookies, Grandpa would make sure to invite her to those things as well. She had always been there for him over the years, so I imagine he wanted to return the favor.

Grandpa passed away in the midst of the coronavirus pandemic. For some time, many of us had avoided visiting for fear of potentially infecting him, but that lost time is something I think we all truly regret. I was fortunate enough to have visited him just a few days before he passed away, which I will always be grateful for, but I still have remorse for all the opportunities I missed to spend more time with him. I do thank God that I was able to take that last bike ride with him and share one last warm embrace, but it's never enough. Honestly, I don't think we can ever have enough time with those we love.

We always thought Grandpa was invincible and that he would be with us forever, but the sad truth is that everyone will eventually leave this world, and nobody can be certain of when that time will come. There are so many people who have lost loved ones far too soon, people who would give anything for just one more hug or another "I love you." I think most would say that it is always too soon when a loved one leaves us which is why I believe we should be incredibly grateful for the time that we do have with them. So before you put off visiting a loved one or make some excuse for not calling home more often, take a moment to recognize how much your family loves you and how much joy you bring to their lives. Think about all the sacrifices they have made for you over the years and consider returning the favor every now and then. Even a quick phone call to check in can mean the world to them.

I have been blessed with an incredible family who has helped me recognize the power of unconditional love, so my heart genuinely aches for those who have not had a similar upbringing or for those who take their families for granted. Family should be a place where you always feel accepted and valued, people you can turn to no matter what, and a constant source of love and support. In my opinion, the bond of a family should never be broken over a petty argument or a disagreement that caused someone hurt. Instead, family is something that should be fought for and a place where forgiveness is given freely.

I realize that not everyone grew up in a tight-knit family as I did and that some were even born orphans, not knowing who their true parents or family were. Again, my heart breaks for these individuals because I believe that everyone deserves a place where they feel loved and accepted no matter what. I just hope that if you know someone who is in this position, that you could take on that role of "family" and be that source of unconditional love and support for them because nobody deserves to go through this life alone.

Grandpa cherished his family and put us first in everything. He recognized how valuable family is and made sure to always honor that special bond. Whether he was surrounded by family for a holiday celebration or simply sitting on the back porch with a few loved ones, he never took that time for granted because he knew those moments would not last forever. The truth is, we can never get back the opportunities we miss to spend time with our loved ones, and while in the moment it may seem inconvenient or you may feel as though you have something better to do, I believe that the most valuable way you can spend your time is in the presence of family. I understand that life can get in the way of this sometimes and that your schedule may not always allow for it, but I simply want to encourage you to be intentional about making time for those who love you most. Appreciate your loved ones and show them how much they mean to you because you never know when you will no longer have that opportunity.

Life Lesson #11:

Make family a priority because the bond of a family is something to be cherished. Be there for one another, support each other, and love one another unconditionally.

Rule #12
Choose Love

Grandpa died of what the doctors determined to be a heart attack. Many, though, speculated that he had died of a broken heart, as not only had he lost his wife of 67 years just six months prior, but the isolation that he'd endured through the first several months of the coronavirus pandemic had deprived him of the family time he treasured. Yes, he had expressed how deeply he missed his beloved Leona, and I admit that I too had attributed his passing to a broken heart. However, my Aunt Stacey had an entirely different explanation for what had induced his heart attack, and as she somehow summoned the strength to share this sentiment with us during the funeral service, we all came to a mutual understanding of what had truly happened. She said that Grandpa's heart had burst because there was too much love fighting to get out, and it simply could not contain it any longer.

It was true - Grandpa's heart was overflowing with love for everyone. His genuine smile, his kind interactions, the way in which he constantly put others first - his presence always radiated love, unconditional love at that. I think this was another reason Grandpa had such a powerful influence on others. His love was always genuine and sincere, regardless of who you were. It didn't matter your age, race, religion, sexuality, or past - he was going to treat you with kindness and respect because in his mind, that was always the right thing to do. Just as the saying goes - "you can catch more flies with honey than vinegar" - Grandpa recognized that if you want to make a positive difference in the lives of others, love is the most powerful tool.

Most people make countless connections with others on any given day, and regardless of the intent of that interaction, I'd like to think that most people would choose to approach one another in a kind and respectful manner. Unfortunately, though, I feel as though too many of these interactions are approached with a negative mentality whether it's prejudice, animosity, resentment, or simply indifference. It honestly saddens me to see how much anger and hatred there is in our world today. It feels as though every time I turn on the news there is another story of violence, oftentimes stemming from prejudices against a certain group of people or anger that has arisen from something small and petty. I hear of threats and even attacks against schools and other organizations that have been established to give back to the community. Simply scrolling through social media, one will most likely encounter any number of negative or derogatory comments made toward others, and oftentimes, these comments are unprovoked and directed at complete strangers. I know there is still a lot of love in this world, but unfortunately, there seems to be a lot of opposition as well.

When I see yet another story of this hate or negative commentary meant to degrade another person, I often question where this type of attitude toward others stems from because when you watch young children interact with one another, there doesn't seem to be any prejudice or hatred in their hearts. We aren't born with these feelings, so what causes them to develop?

I sometimes wonder what a person must have gone through in life for them to become so negative, oppositional, or in some cases, downright heartless. I question why some people seem to resort to lives filled with crime, violence, and conflict - hurting others to gain things for themselves. I also wonder why there are children out there who are struggling with depression and suicidal thoughts when this stage of life should be carefree and filled with fun and happiness. There seems to be so much unnecessary hurt and pain in this world today, but why? Unfortunately, I think a reason for this is that too many people have not been shown the love that they deserve, especially in those critical moments of development, and as a result, their hearts become hardened or even worse, they begin to think they are not worthy of love. This honestly breaks my heart. We all started out as innocent infants who are worthy and deserving of love, but sadly, we don't all receive this much-needed affection. I recognize that we all have certain character traits that influence our personalities and ultimately, the way we interact with others, so a lack of love may not always be the explanation, but I do know that a little love can go a long way. Although we can't control what has happened to someone in the past, we can do our part to ensure that our interactions leave them feeling valued and respected.

Now, I know that love is most often thought of as a strong emotion that we only feel for family, friends, and romantic partners, but it's important to remember that love is not just a feeling; it is also an action that can be demonstrated in meaningful ways and can have such a positive impact on others. Fortunately, though, loving others does not require extravagant gestures or significant time; rather, by simply maintaining certain key practices, one can display an incredible amount of love to everyone they encounter.

The first of these, I believe, is the ability to remain open-minded. I was watching an episode of the Apple TV series *Ted Lasso* once when the main character, played by Jason Sudeikis, quoted the great Walt Whitman. He said, "Be curious, not judgmental," and that line has stuck with me ever since because I believe there is so much value in this statement. Oftentimes, we do not know the true background of the person we are so quick to judge. We only see the outward appearance and make assumptions about them based on the few details we do know. We don't consider the hardships they've faced in the past or the inner battles they may be silently fighting on a daily basis. Temperament and outward appearance are influenced by any number of things, but there is so much more to a person than what the eye can see. This life can be tough, especially mentally and emotionally, and those are scars that most people don't wear on their sleeves. So rather than judging someone who looks, speaks, thinks, or acts differently than us, we should be curious and try to understand why they are the way they are. Obviously we don't want to be nosy, but through light-hearted yet genuine conversation, you can truly learn a lot about a person and show them a little love in the process. Furthermore, you may discover something that changes your own perspective and allows you to respect and potentially even appreciate those differences.

Remaining open-minded is a great first step towards displaying love, but I believe we can always take it a step further and empathize with others as well. It's one thing to sympathize and feel sorry for them, but empathy creates a much more powerful and supportive connection. You don't need to experience the exact same situation in order to show them a little compassion, though; rather, by "putting yourself in their shoes" and seeing the situation from their perspective, it can help you better understand what they are going through and provide greater insight into their unique story.

I recognize that empathy can be a difficult emotion to express as it does require a certain degree of selflessness. It means setting aside your own views and experiences in order to fully grasp what another person is going through. In my experience, people want to feel heard; they want to feel valued and respected, but when we are too busy trying to be right or forcing our own ideas on them, we end up making them feel as though their thoughts and feelings don't matter. Although we may feel as though we are just trying to help and do not intend to belittle a person's ideas or emotions, it can still cause a person to feel incredibly small, especially to someone who is already lacking confidence. This type of interaction may seem insignificant to some, but to somebody who experiences this type of feeling over and over again, it can really take a toll on their mental and emotional well-being which, in turn, could have potentially devastating consequences. However, when we approach them with compassion and understanding, this will leave them feeling valued and loved, and honestly, you would be surprised at the impact that this type of interaction can have on someone struggling with their self-worth. Speaking from personal experience, it can mean the world to them.

Finally, I think kindness and respect are two of the most basic yet most important qualities when it comes to love. Think about it - we get to decide how we will treat others and interact with them, so we can either choose to be kind or we can choose to be hateful, but what does one gain from the latter? Maybe putting others down makes you feel as though you are better than them or it boosts your ego for a moment, but I assure you, most people are going to think less of you when you take this approach.

Now, I understand that some people are difficult to love, especially when all they've ever done is bully, belittle, or take advantage of you. Oftentimes, though, I believe those are the people that need love the most. I know it can be challenging to be kind to those who have done you wrong, but if you think about it, the way you treat others is a reflection of you more so than them. We can control how we interact with others, so we can either choose to be petty and rude or we can choose to take the high road and not allow ourselves to feed into their negativity. I had a boss once who would always say, "Kill 'em with kindness." Now, this does not necessarily mean giving them what they want simply to please them, but it does mean approaching them in a kind and patient manner. Some people may think this is a sign of weakness, but I disagree. I think it takes so much more strength and discipline to remain respectful in trying situations than to lose your temper or become combative. It is incredibly difficult to remain calm, cool, and collected as someone insults and berates you, but I believe that in doing so, you will prove yourself to be the bigger person, and furthermore, you won't give them the satisfaction of falling into their trap.

Have you ever noticed the amount of love and support that pours out following a tragedy. I consider the moments after a devastating tornado tears through a neighborhood when people from all over the country gather to help clean up and provide much-needed resources. I think of the days following the sudden death of a beloved community member when neighbors stop by with casseroles and offer assistance in any way they can. These times seem to bring people together and remind us of the love we have for one another.

I still remember the days and weeks following the horror of September 11th, 2001 - despite the overwhelming feelings of fear and sadness that blanketed the country, the people of our nation came together like never before. The sense of unity was palpable as everyone seemed to set their differences aside to offer one another support. People treated others with kindness and understanding as patriotism took precedence over politics for a change.

More recently, I was watching the Monday Night football game when Damar Hamlin of the Buffalo

Bills took a hit to the chest and went into cardiac arrest right there on the field. As the people in the stadium and viewers across the country waited and prayed in fearful silence, there was an overwhelming sense of love and genuine concern for humankind. In that moment, it seemed as though everyone recognized the value of a person and realized that no amount of money an NFL game generates or the weight a game holds in the run for playoffs is worth a life. Every football fan and person who watched the news of the terrifying play rallied around Hamlin, following his progress and cheering for his recovery. The outpouring of love and support during this time was incredible, and although I would never want anyone to go through what Hamlin and his family experienced that night, I truly believe that God was using this moment to send a greater message. Even before his on-field scare, Hamlin was all about spreading love in this world. From the heart sign he would always make with his hands to his inspiring messages of love, it is evident that his purpose extends far beyond the football field. Although it was probably not the platform that he had envisioned, this frightening experience has allowed him to share his message of love with an even greater audience - a message that I feel needs to be shared now more than ever.

I admit that my inspiration for the title of this chapter came from the message that not only Hamlin, but many NFL players used to wear on the back of their helmets. I love watching football, and although the way the game is played does not necessarily demonstrate love, I am always inspired by the work the league, teams, and individual players do to support meaningful causes in their communities and around the world. I especially appreciate the social justice messages that were approved to be displayed on players' helmets beginning in the 2021 season. These messages have included "stop hate," "end racism," "it takes all of us," and "inspire change," but "choose love" has always been my favorite because I believe it encompasses all of these important messages in just two simple words.

I truly believe that no matter how much darkness there is in this world, there is an even greater abundance of kindness, compassion, and generosity. It may seem harder to find at times, but it's out there, everywhere, we just need to look for it. Unfortunately, I think far too often we give too much attention to the hate in this world. Consider the daily news and the countless stories that are shared of violence, crime, and opposition in this world, and although they may leave you with a happy story at the end of the broadcast, it feels as though the bad usually outweighs the good. I wonder, though, what would happen if our newsfeeds shared more stories about people doing good and spreading love - would that inspire others to do the same?

I'm not saying that love is non-existent in this world, but sometimes it seems to pale in comparison to the amount of love that emerges following tragedies and other catastrophes. Unfortunately, there are always going to be haters and people who use any excuse to push their own agendas, but in these moments, those critics are always silenced by the resounding displays of love. Just imagine if our love for one another was always this strong - we could potentially silence their voices altogether. The love is there, so rather than waiting for a tragic reason to show it, I want to encourage you to look for ways to spread a little love each and every day. Again, this does not require in-depth conversations or grand gestures; rather, it's as simple as treating others with kindness and respect. Smiling at strangers as you pass them on the sidewalk, saying "please" and "thank you" to the barista as they make your morning coffee, or waiting a couple extra seconds to hold the door open for someone who is just a few steps behind you - these simple acts can go a long way. I also challenge you to step out of your comfort zone once in a while and start a simple conversation with somebody who you never really paid much attention to or an individual who is different from those you typically interact with. Consider that person who rides the same train as you every morning or that person at work who always keeps to themselves. This may seem like an odd thing to do, especially when these days many people seem to be glued to their phones in an attempt to avoid any eye contact or interaction with strangers, but I think this type of human connection is something this world desperately needs. By having these conversations and genuinely showing interest in others, not only do they feel valued, but we gain a greater understanding of humankind and are able to develop a more well-rounded worldview. This, in turn, allows us to better respect and appreciate differences and ultimately, love others more.

Love is a powerful thing. It can soften hearts that

have been hardened by years of neglect and rejection. For those who feel as though they have nothing to offer, love can help them feel valued and encouraged. Love generates a lot of good in this world and the best part is it is free to give and simple to offer. The more we keep an open mind and treat others with kindness, compassion, and respect, the more we will spread some of that much-needed love in this world.

Life Lesson #12:

There is no limit to the amount of love you can give, so choose love always because love always wins.

Rule #13
Enjoy the Ride

People respected and admired Grandpa for many reasons, but the thing that he was probably most known for was his presence on the Buffalo Valley Rail Trail.

Before I was even born, Grandpa had undergone triple bypass surgery, and the doctor reminded him often of the importance of regular exercise. Unfortunately, walking was difficult for him as his knees and hips were worn from years of hard labor, so my uncles, who are both avid mountain bikers themselves, thought bike-riding might be a good option, and boy, were they right. Grandpa fell in love with it, and when the township converted an old railroad track into a bike path, his passion for the activity grew even more.

My grandparents' house sits about one mile from the start of the trail which then extends nine miles from their hometown to the town of Lewisburg, so a round trip totaled a little more than 20 miles for Grandpa. He made this trek as often as he could, and not even the wind or rain would deter him from getting in his ride. He wouldn't always do the full twenty, but I would say he averaged at least 10 to 15 miles per trip. He would always record the number of miles he biked following each ride, and when we found this log after he had passed, we discovered that he had ridden over 1,100 miles on that trail in just a little over 3 months. In fact, he had just ridden the full 20-mile round trip the day before he passed away.

Grandpa loved riding that rail trail, not only for the freedom and fresh air the ride offered, but also for the people he met along the way. As much as he enjoyed riding his bike, I believe he enjoyed the connections and conversations he had with the other "Rail Trail Regulars" even more so. As typically happens in a small town, he had come to know many of the locals over the years, so he crossed paths with familiar faces often. Many times he would stop to chat with them to ask how they were doing and catch up on town news. He had made some new friends over the years as well, befriending individuals he most likely never would have met had it not been for the new bike path. It didn't matter if he had known you for 30 years or 30 minutes, though; he would treat you as though you were his best friend.

Grandpa was essentially famous to those who frequented the rail trail. The local newspaper had even written a story about him, highlighting his passion for biking and the countless miles he logged on the trail. As were most people who passed by Grandpa as he pedaled along, the journalists at the paper were just as impressed that an 85-year-old man would be so motivated and even capable of riding his bike as much as he did. As a family, we were excited for him to get this recognition; however, based on the photo that had been taken and displayed along with the article, Grandpa was not so thrilled to be in the spotlight. In fact, he appeared quite unhappy in the picture, and I'm sure some people even questioned his passion for bike riding as they read it, but this was just another testament to his humility. He didn't ride his bike to impress others or gain their attention and adulation - instead, he rode his bike for him and the way it made him feel. I saw a quote once that I feel best describes his love of biking; it read: "I don't ride my bike to win races, nor do I ride to get places. I ride to escape this world. I ride to find peace with myself. I ride to feel free, and I ride to feel strong." (Anonymous). When he was on his bike, he was simply enjoying the ride.

A few weeks after Grandpa had passed, my Uncle Scot was riding the trail, when he noticed a new sign had been posted on one of the mile markers. As he got nearer and was able to make out the script, he immediately came to a halt as he read the words "Ed Wagner Memorial Highway." As he shared his discovery with everyone, our family was overwhelmed with gratitude for this display of recognition and desperately wanted to thank the person behind this kind and thoughtful gesture. They first contacted the trail authority, but we quickly learned that the mystery person hadn't asked permission to hang the sign, so they couldn't provide any information; however, to our delight, they did agree that the sign would remain posted. After the first attempt came up empty, my mom and her siblings continued the search, individually asking anyone they thought might be responsible, posting updates on Facebook, and inquiring around his church, but it was to no avail. Although I was just as curious as the rest of my family to discover who the kind-hearted person was behind this act, I remember thinking how remarkable it was that they had orchestrated this memorial in the same manner as Grandpa would have - humbly and not seeking any recognition or praise.

It was not until more than a year later that we finally learned the identity of the individual responsible for the sign, and ironically, it was someone we would have never expected. Although he was still hesitant to reveal his good deed, he had been encouraged by my Uncle Scot's boss because he knew how much our family wanted to express our gratitude. Reluctantly, the man approached my Uncle Scot at the bike shop where he works one day and shared that he did not know Grandpa personally but he would pass by him on the trail frequently. He said that he had always been inspired by Grandpa's passion for riding the rail trail, and he felt that dedication needed to be commemorated.

My family was so grateful that we were finally able to personally thank the man for his incredible gift, but even more so, I think we were in awe that it was someone to whom Grandpa had never even spoken. Grandpa touched the lives of many, but this sentiment just goes to show that one can have an impact on others even simply in passing. I don't think we can ever truly know the impact we have on others, but that is why it is so important to make sure our actions and interactions are always positive because you never know who is watching and what kind of mark you are making on this world.

My family now rides the rail trail, honoring Grandpa's passion for biking and celebrating the legacy that he has left behind, and as I pedal along during these rides, I have come to understand why Grandpa loved riding the trail so much. It's definitely a workout, especially for an 88-year-old man, but it's not so strenuous that it has you wishing it was over. Rather, it's a peaceful ride that provides an escape from this world. Surrounded by beautiful scenery and people enjoying the fresh air, you get all the benefits that nature has to offer.

I often wonder what Grandpa would think about as he pedaled along that trail, mile after mile. I could be wrong, but if I know Grandpa, I imagine he wasn't thinking about much at all. Rather, he was simply embracing the moment, thankful for the opportunity to do what he loved. The light breeze hitting his face, the sweet scent of the wildflowers swaying back and forth along the path, the birds chirping and the laughter of children playing at the park - I envision him taking it all in and being grateful for every last detail, even the unpleasant odor that often emanated from the cow farm that sits alongside the trail.

Thoughts of his family most likely crossed his mind during these rides as well, reminiscing and cherishing the life he had built with the wife he adored. I'm sure he thought about his five children and relished in their successes and the way they had each grown into confident, kind, and caring individuals. I imagine he thought of his grandchildren and great grandchildren as well, pondering their futures and hoping that life would be as good to them as it had been to him. I can't say for certain that this is what he would think about as he traveled the trail, but I'm sure that whatever his thoughts were, they were full of gratitude as well as a sense of peace.

Have you ever considered where your thoughts tend to wander throughout the day? For me, I often find myself worrying about everything I need to do in the upcoming days, dwelling on situations that are bothering me, or even trying to plan out the rest of my day, week, or even life. However, I realize that these thoughts are ultimately just added stress. Worrying about all I need to do isn't accomplishing the tasks, dwelling on upsetting situations is only causing me greater angst, and as the saying goes, plans are made to be broken. I find it so challenging to simply be in the moment and embrace where I am, but I know that this type of mentality would certainly be a breath of fresh air.

Nowadays, we seem to live in a society where we are constantly rushing from one thing to the next. We fill our schedules with work, social events, and other countless activities, always trying to get ahead and rarely allowing ourselves any downtime. I'm not saying that these are bad things and that we shouldn't be social or goal-oriented; however, I think that this type of lifestyle doesn't always grant us the opportunity to "stop and smell the roses". Sometimes we are so focused on where we are going that we forget to appreciate the path that is leading us there, and in my opinion, the journey is just as important as the final destination.

I think John Lennon put it best when he said, "Life is what happens when you're busy making other plans." Too often we let special moments slip by us because our minds are preoccupied with other things. Obviously, life does require a certain degree of planning, otherwise, not much would ever get accomplished. However, I do encourage you to live in the moment as much as possible and find joy in even the most basic happenings because these times are still so important. Be grateful for those moments when you're playing cards with your family or chatting with them around the dinner table or even those times when your kids are whining in the back seat, saying "Are we there yet?" because one day you will look back and miss those moments. Life is unpredictable. You never know when that last conversation or hug will be or when you'll take your last bike ride, so embrace each and every moment you are given.

I recognize that some rides are smoother than others, but no matter how many mountains you need to climb, they are still a part of your journey, and in my opinion, those mountains only make the story more interesting and reaching the final destination that much sweeter. Unfortunately, life isn't always easy, and sometimes it throws us curve balls that in the moment, we may feel we will never overcome. The ability to do so, though, leads to greater growth, and that growth is something to be grateful for. So even in those toughest of times, try to find the silver lining and make the best out of the situation because I don't know about you, but I want my story to be about strength and resilience rather than defeat.

Grandpa rode his bike the same way he lived his life - embracing every moment. He recognized that life is a gift, and it should never be taken for granted. So remember to not only live in the moment as much as possible but also to appreciate each and every moment you are given because none of it is guaranteed. Be grateful for the journey life is taking you on - it is all a part of your story, so make it one you are proud to share.

Life Lesson #13:

You only get one life to live so make the most out of it. Pursue your dreams, love freely, and do what makes you happy, but most importantly, enjoy the ride.

Epilogue
Rule #14: Be Good.

"He didn't tell me how to live; he lived and let me watch him do it."

-Clarence Budington Kelland

After every visit to my grandparents' house, as I would be getting ready to leave, Grandma would always say to me, "Be good."

I would simply respond with a smile and say, "I always am."

And when Grandma was no longer well enough to say these parting words, Grandpa continued the tradition, always reminding me to be good as I walked out the door. Growing up, it just seemed like a routine to me - something people would say as they were parting ways. However, looking back on it, I now understand the purpose and the sentiment behind those two little words.

I'm sure there are many hopes and aspirations that grandparents have for their grandchildren - for them to be loved, to find success in their endeavors, and for them to be happy and healthy, all of which are great things to strive for. But as I consider my grandparents' parting words and regular reminders to "be good," I have come to realize what was most important to them: that their grandchildren be good people.

I know that I am far from perfect, but I would like to think that I am a good person for the most part. Fortunately for me, I had a pretty remarkable role model, and although I may never achieve the bar that Grandpa has set, I will forever be grateful for the life lessons I have learned simply by watching him. Even as I wrote this book, I was able to gain a greater understanding of his ways and the qualities that made him so extraordinary. He was and is an inspiration, not only to me, but to so many because he truly was a light in this world. I'm sure we all have people we admire and different reasons as to why they are our heroes. For me, that person was Grandpa because he showed me what it means to be a good person, which in my opinion, is one of the greatest things we can achieve in our lifetime.

Although I can't say for certain what the secret is to a life well lived, I do know that Grandpa held the key to it. He was a man of incredible integrity and discipline which allowed him to maintain his values no matter what this world threw at him. I think there were a lot of factors that helped him achieve this, from his small-town mindset and humble upbringing to his steadfast faith, but ultimately, I believe the essence of his character can be summed up in a single word: *love*. Like my Aunt Stacey said, his heart was overflowing with it - love for himself, love for others, and a love for life. Because of this, he radiated a special kind of light, one that attracted others and brightened their days. Whether you were a stranger or a lifelong friend, he was a helping hand in times of need, and just being in his presence gave you a sense of peace and comfort. He was a source of unconditional love for everyone and everything, and I believe that is what truly allowed him to have such an incredible impact on those around him.

Now, I recognize that everyone has a different life story as we all have a unique background and personal experiences that have influenced us, and thus, shaped our own set of beliefs and guiding principles by which we aim to live. You may have a different definition of what it means to be a good person, and I respect that. I simply wanted to share some of the qualities that I recognized in Grandpa who was one of the best people I have ever known. The rules that I have shared are certainly not the ultimate guide to achieving a good life, but I do know that it was because of these principles that Grandpa was able to leave this world a better place. And as I've reflected on his life, I am reminded of the fact that it doesn't take fame or wealth to leave behind a lasting legacy. You don't need to lead movements or preach to large crowds to have a positive impact. Like Gandhi said, "Be the change you wish to see in the world." Simply embodying the qualities that you value most will allow you to be a positive example for others, and this is exactly what Grandpa did. Through his character which guided his actions, he was able to create small ripples of love in this world, ripples that have empowered those around him to do the same.

Each and every day, we have the opportunity to make a difference in this world, either positive or negative. Fortunately, we get to make that decision by choosing the type of person we are going to be. The truth is, how we interact with this world is a choice, and we all have the power to choose kindness and love over selfishness and hate. Some days may be more difficult than others as the ways of this world can be overwhelming at times, but the good news is that each day can be a fresh start. Even if we do stumble, the following day, we get to choose to be better than we were the day before.

Let me ask you this: How do you want to be remembered? In my experience, eulogies often focus on one's character traits rather than their looks, wealth, or possessions because a person's legacy is built on who they are, not what they have. Ultimately, it is your character that inspires others, not your outward appearance or lifestyle. Therefore, I believe that if you truly want to leave an enduring impression, one that touches the lives of others and encourages them to do the same, you need to make sure your heart is in the right place.

I genuinely believe that most people are good. The challenge, though, is to make it a habit. Let's face it - we're all human, and we all fall into the traps that society lays for us. I admit that even Grandpa had his moments when he let this world get the best of him, but the key is to not let these moments define us. Rather, we must recognize these times as opportunities for growth, learning from past mistakes in order to become a better person. I realize that doing the right thing is not always easy - it takes a tremendous amount of self-control, but I do know it is possible because I witnessed it firsthand in Grandpa.

Everybody has the power within them to be a good person. The discipline one needs to consistently choose good is not going to develop overnight, and some days will be better than others, but ultimately, I think you will find that people will respect and appreciate you that much more when you allow that goodness to guide your life. It certainly takes integrity to withstand the negative ways of this world, but if you have a little love in your heart, then you have the capacity to do it. Just imagine a world in which everyone chose gratitude, compassion, and love over greed, ego, and hate. Now that is the kind of world I want to live in.

So I leave you with this final rule: Be good. Be good to yourself, and be good to others because good people are what make this world a better place. And as you aspire to be a good person, I challenge you to embrace each and every day as an opportunity to be better than you were the day before. You only get one life to live, so shouldn't you live it to the fullest, striving to be the best person you can possibly be?

Whether or not you choose to incorporate some of "Grandpa's Rules" into your own life (if you don't already), I hope that you will at least be encouraged to be a good person. Consider what it means to you to "be good," and then, let that character guide your life always. I hope that you recognize your value and the influence you can have on others. Don't ever doubt the power of your love and the impact it can have on this world. Just like Grandpa, you, too, can leave a lasting legacy that inspires others by simply embracing a lifestyle guided by those two little words: Be Good.

Life Lesson #14:

Be good, and let your goodness be the spark that
brings out the goodness in others.